I've personally kno........................ce the early 1980s. I have witnessed .... for Jesus. H........ ad His people. I am grateful for her faithfulness and humility and how she unashamedly sang and taught the Scriptures to bring life to her own spirit and to those around her. She helped us birth IHOP-KC and served faithfully as a worship leader, pastor, leader, and trainer of young prophetic singers and musicians. I am so grateful for her love and labor over so many years. Her new book represents her life-long journey filled with life-giving insight and real-life application derived from her lifelong dedication to being a student of the Word just like David was. She is the real deal.

—Mike Bickle
International House of Prayer

Julie Meyer is a trusted prophetess, psalmist, and mentor, stellar in both character and gifting. This book will change your life as you are taught, empowered, and motivated to sing the Psalms. Things will shift in your life as a result. I highly endorse Julie and the life message she has penned in this book. Buy one for your friends too—they will treasure it as a precious, life-transforming gift.

—Patricia King
Author, Christian Minister, TV Host

I have heard it stated that some say prayers, some are consistent in prayer, and a few become prayer itself. I believe the same can be true about praise and worship as well. Some do praise, others become persistent in praise, and a few become the embodiment of praise itself. What would the believer look and act like if these two strategic spiritual warfare components were brought together within their very own lifestyle? Yes, into the very fabric of their personhood?

That is what my friend, Julie Meyer, aims to be and demonstrate in and through her life. That is what the Lord's singing servant attempts to produce in others—the true convergence of prayer and praise who wears the seamless garment of the ministering priest and the trumpeting prophet. Julie Meyer gives you effective keys to equip you for battle in her book, *30 Days of Praying the Psalms*. Don't just read this book. I dare you to practice it!

With Delightful Joy,
—James W. Goll
Founder of God Encounters Ministries
GOLL Ideation, LLC

Amazing! A month filled with glory as you read *30 Days of Praying the Psalms!* And who better than Julie Meyer, a modern-day psalmist who sings like an angel and writes like a poet. This engaging devotional will keep you soaking in God's presence and singing in splendor. I found something released inside of me as I read through this masterpiece. You honestly need to read this and soar with high praises on the rocket of prayer. You'll find each day focusing on a psalm and a prayer. I wish every believer would spend a month with this book. I know you will enjoy it!

—Brian Simmons
The Passion Translation Project

We love it when Julie Meyer is able to minister in Succat Hallel. Julie Meyer is truly a laid-down lover of God who keeps evergreen in her love relationship with the Lord. And her passion is contagious. I love the way she pursues God without getting religious. Every time she sings or shares, I sense it comes out of a treasure chest of which we are only seeing one of the hundreds of gold coins contained there.

This is not just a book, but this is *life* that is the overflow of her life of ministering to the Lord. And this book and the songs that come with it will lead you to soar with Julie like an eagle above your circumstances, seeing from a third-heaven viewpoint that magnifies God and puts the rest of life into the right perspective. Enjoy!

—Rick Ridings
Founder, Succat Hallel
24/7 House of Prayer overlooking the Temple Mount
in Jerusalem, Israel
Author, *Shifting Nations Through Houses of Prayer*

Julie Meyer had written an exquisite book! *30 Days of Praying the Psalms* is rich and will add a depth to your daily devotions that will give you a new intimacy with Christ.

—Cindy Jacobs
Generals International

Julie Meyer is one of the most unique, fun, creative, godly, and out-of-the-box people I know. *30 Days of Praying the Psalms* so represents Julie. I love the Psalms. She brings them down to earth, makes them practical, and even teaches us how to glean lessons from them. I have heard her sing and pray the Psalms. My spirit reaches out for her every word! She brings them alive, teaching us how to do the same. Julie is a master at her craft, which is worship and intercession, praying the Word while playing on her instrument. She is truly one filled with a heart like David. You'll love and savor this book! It's *heart!*

—Barbara J. Yoder
Lead Apostle, Shekinah
Regional Apostolic Center
www.shekinahchurch.org

Of anyone I've ever met, I doubt any other person has sung more of the Psalms than my own mother. Who better to learn from of its benefits? Here, she breathes, quite literally, new life into the ancient practice of singing the Psalms, distilling her approach into a simple daily practice that all stand to grow from.

—Jesse Meyer
Julie's son

My friend, Julie Meyer, has been singing, praying, and living the Psalms even before I knew her. This book is simply the overflow of her life obsession—of dwelling in the courts of the Lord to gaze on Him and inquire of Him. Nobody knows how to sing the Psalms more skillfully or impart their significance more meaningfully. Get Julie at her best!

—Bob Sorge
Author, *Secrets of the Secret Place*

I challenge you to change your life! *30 Days of Praying the Psalms* will give you what you have been longing for. Real tools you can use in your day-to-day life to bring about lasting change. This book will encourage you to take God's Word and let it mold you more into His image.

—Rick and Lori Taylor
Directors of Santa Maria Apostolic Center

30 Days of Praying the Psalms, like everything my friend Julie Meyer does, is simple, heartfelt, powerful, and life changing. Rather than a traditional devotional guide, this is an assisted journey into an experiential, spiritual realm of encounters with God as you soak in the presence of the Almighty. Julie's work combines beautiful music with insightful spiritual words to search out the deep things of God in the places of greatest human need through the songs of David. You will love this experience and I expect that you will want to read each section several times. I have no doubt that you will want to share this with your friends too.

Thank you, Julie Meyer, for continually leading us to the throne of grace!

—Joan Hunter
Author, Evangelist
TV host: *Miracles Happen*

The Hebrew Psalms contain ubiquitous observations about society, justice, defeat, and vindication with which anyone from anywhere can relate. However, there are challenges for a modern reader who tries to access their value under the layers of translated poetry from a largely unspoken language (or two since she is also writing about the Septuagint), shrouded by millennia, and potentially living thousands of miles whence they were first sung. However, with simple prose undergirded by a devotional life spanning decades (both in public and in private), my mother's book will help connect readers to ancient insights from our religious ancestors as if they were sung by contemporary poets.

—Joseph Meyer (Julie's Son)
Ph.D. Fellow in Classical Languages & Literature

The Psalms is the most quoted book on social media and the book that the New Testament cites most frequently. The reason for this, as Julie Meyer so wonderfully teaches in this book, is that the Psalms give us divinely inspired language to speak to God honestly about our victories and losses. Armed with this language, you too will be able to overcome the pain and disappointment that life throws at you. And I can assure you, Julie has not written this book out of her head, but rather as a person who has faithfully practiced the singing of the Psalms for decades and who has discovered the overcoming power of daily praying the Psalms. I highly recommend it!

—Stacey Campbell
Shiloh Global
wesleystaceycampbell.com

Julie Meyer is always seeking after the heart of God, so Julie is one of the brightest kingdom lights I know. Julie, like the psalmist David of old, has learned the secret of entering into God's courts with thanksgiving and maintaining God's presence in her life through her continuous worship, adoration, and high praises. This amazing book will empower you to discover the face of God through daily receiving, living, and adapting the kingdom principles found in *30 Days of Praying the Psalms*. Like Julie, you too will become an intimate friend of God with whom He shares His dreams and secrets. When you read and apply these life-changing biblical principles to your life, you will gladly rejoice in the goodness of the Lord, tap into His strength, and gain the power needed to overcome any obstacle to live a successful, abundant life in the land of the living.

—Dr. Barbie L. Breathitt
President of Breath of the Spirit Ministries, Inc.
DreamsDecoder.com
Author of *Dream Interpreter* and many more

I have always admired the ministry of Julie Meyer. She is a true worshiper who carries the presence of God with a passion for believers to become wholehearted worshipers. Julie's book, *30 Days of Praying the Psalms*, will cause these precious psalms to come alive within you as you meditate and pray through each one. With each psalm, Julie shares the revelations that she has gleaned from the heart of God. Enjoy this wonderful book as I have!

—Ryan Bruss
Author *of Carrying the Presence* and *Living Loved*

Julie's passion for the Word of God is both convicting and contagious. In this book, Julie articulates the message of the Book of Psalms in such a captivating and understandable way. Her ability to pull you into the heart of the story and help you apply its truth to your own life is a gift. For anyone wanting a deeper relationship with the Lord and further understanding of the power of His Word at work in your life, this book is for you.

—Catherine Mullins
Speaker, Songwriter, and Worship Artist
www.catherinemullins.com
Never Lost A Battle

We love Julie Meyer, and it is always such a delight to read her books because just like her, they are full of Jesus. One thing we've learned is that when you spend time around people who love Jesus, it creates a deeper passion inside of you. There is a real, tangible anointing that is transferred into your life. And the same thing happens when you read Julie's books. In reading *30 Days of Praying the Psalms,* we found the Psalms coming alive inside of us, and we believe the same thing will happen for you, too! Julie writes from a place of deep revelation and personal experience. Let her share these secrets from the psalms with you. By the time you finish reading this book, you will be changed. We highly recommend the life, ministry, and writings of Julie Meyer and we're delighted to call her our friend.

—Joshua and Janet Mills
International Glory Ministries
www.joshuamills.com

Spiritual warfare is real, and it's not a coincidence that you're looking at this book! I can personally attest to many times when I felt like I was in a thick war against the enemy, that worship with the Word of God and praise was the thing that helped me find breakthrough the most! Julie Meyer has given us such a gift in this book, *30 Days of Praying the Psalms*. She unpacks the prophetic symbolism as well as the reference to the meaning behind what King David wrote in the Psalms as he warred against Saul. The Psalms are *keys* to the Kingdom! This book unlocks keys to breakthrough warfare!

—Ana Werner
Founder of Ana Werner Ministries
President, Eagles Network
Author and Prophetic Seer
www.anawerner.org

30 Days
of Praying the

Psalms

King David's
Keys for Victory

JULIE MEYER

DESTINY IMAGE BOOKS BY JULIE MEYER

Dreams and Supernatural Encounters

Dedication

I dedicate this book to my Dad, Randy Hupe. My dad has stayed steady and true throughout the decades. Dad, you meet each day with a smile no matter what life tends to surprise you with. You remind me of the tree in Psalm 1. All through the storms of life, you bend, you bow, you stand strong, you forgive, you believe the best about people, *(which is rare in these days)* you laugh, and you read the Psalms. You are one of the best and most committed givers that I know. I love our phone calls when you ask me if I have read Psalm 94? Or if I have read Psalm 91? You are an inspiration to me and to every one of your children and their wives and husbands and their children and their children. I mean, you are 81 years young and still when I post your picture on social media, I get 25 messages asking if you are single. You know, you just gotta' love a Dad like that. Thank you for being so amazing. I want to be like you. I love you, Dad.

DESTINY IMAGE® PUBLISHERS, INC.
P.O. Box 310, Shippensburg, PA 17257-0310
"Promoting Inspired Lives."

This book and all other Destiny Image and Destiny Image Fiction books are available at Christian bookstores and distributors worldwide.

Cover design by Eileen Rockwell.

For more information on foreign distributors, call 717-532-3040.

Reach us on the Internet: www.destinyimage.com.

ISBN 13 TP: 978-0-7684-5461-1

ISBN 13 eBook: 978-0-7684-5459-8

ISBN 13 HC: 978-0-7684-5458-1

ISBN 13 LP: 978-0-7684-5460-4

For Worldwide Distribution, Printed in the U.S.A.

1 2 3 4 5 6 7 8 / 25 24 23 22 21

Acknowledgments

I want to thank my amazing husband, Walt, of 36 years. You have spoken the most encouraging words, sometimes at the midnight hour when my writing light in the kitchen woke you up. There you were, maybe grabbing some cheese and crackers, and your words, "Julie, I am proud of you. You can do this." I love you, Walt.

Thank you to Joseph Meyer, whose studies of Ancient Greek and graduating summa cum laude from Santa Barbara University have been such a blessing to me in writing this book. Thank you, Joseph, for a fresh inspiration that sheds light on the Greek language and how it has so beautifully unwrapped words in these Psalms.

Thank you to my amazing, happy Grands, Sophia Grace (Elsa Rebecca Snow) and Shiah Isaac. (Shiah the Fan Man). Oh, how you bring complete delight to my heart. My prayer for you both and all those Grands who are *yet* to be born—may you love the Word of God. May you find yourself within the pages of the Psalms and may these Psalms inspire you and encourage you just like they have me thoughout my life.

Thank you to "My Three Sons" and their amazing wives. Isaac and Brittany, Joseph and Sarah, Jesse and our brand-new daughter in love *Emily*. Emily, what a gift you are to Jesse and our family. I still say this about all three of my daughters in love—Brittany, Sarah and Emily—you are a gift. God hand-picked you for three crazy Meyer boys and I am delighted.

I cannot leave out Luna, Thomas, Molly, and Louisa—we love all of you. We need you in our lives to help us be better humans.

To Mark, Lori Pbert, and David Etzel (*Emily's family*), welcome to the Wild Meyer Wacky World. We are excited to get to know you more and love that we are now *family*. Mark and Lori, thank you for raising such an amazing daughter. I say this to all the parents of my amazing daughters in love. I am so blessed as a mother of boys.

To Isaac Meyer and Joseph Meyer—thank you for all that you do for our Into the River online worship community. We have been recording the Psalms since June 2016, starting with Psalm 1. We are almost halfway through the entire Book, every month recording and releasing Bible studies on the Book of Psalms. What a complete joy it is to work with my sons. (Jesse, I still want an app.) Intotheriver.net

To my family, Penny and Jay—Jay is amazing. We love Jay—and his cooking. Oh my gosh. Jeff and Melodee, your baking and your cakes #amazing. I'm excited about this wedding. Jamie and Doug— Doug, your cooking and your deep fried turkey for Thanksgiving! We love you and we are praying and fighting for healing with you. To all my amazing nieces and nephews: Ashley and Peter (Peter, welcome to the family), Reagan, Lizzy, Brooke, Jenny, Kylee, Colton—I think you all are incredible.

Thank you to our *Julie Meyer Ministries* Board of Directors, Jerry Reardon, Dr. Jeff Earl and Fran Golden. What an encouragement and wealth of knowledge you bring to Walt and me personally. We have truly been lifelong friends and now comrades in ministry. We are honored that you would serve with us.

Rick and Lori Taylor, you are a gift to Santa Maria, CA. You are a gift to me and to my entire family. I continually thank God that I get to do life with you, worship with you, learn and glean mighty faith from you both. I get to see God heal right alongside you. Thank you for who you are, and I thank God that you are *my friends*. But more than that, my children *really* like you a lot. And that means *everything*. You are the real deal, inside and out. I do not think it possible to put into words how much you have impacted my life and my family's life by your kindness, your giving hearts, and your desire to love, give, heal, and bless.

Mike and Diane Bickle, I still remember the day way back in 1983 when Mike told me to go get my Bible, open to the Psalms, sit at my piano, sing, and *never stop*. Well, I didn't. I am still singing the Psalms and singing the Scriptures. Thank you, Mike and Diane, for all that you have poured into me and my entire family. Your love and kindness are such a great gift that it would be impossible to repay you both. I am blessed to always be a part of the international family of IHOP-KC. I love you both.

Graeme and Sabrina Walsh, I have learned from Graeme the incredible joy of "piles of mercy" that is continually available to each of us. Piles and piles and piles of mercy. And Sabrina, when my daughters love you then you are a friend for life. When you sit down and weep with my daughters, that is eternal, Sabrina, that is love and you are the prize. Thank you that you have finally made me Graeme's prophecy partner.

Cindy Gough, you are my twin. And once a twin, always a twin. I treasure all that I have learned from you and all that we will still conquer through Intercession together.

Ryan Bruss, I love it that I get to work with you. You are deep, you are so much fun, you believe for the biggest miracles, and you just help me to believe that too. Thank you. Love that I get to minister with you throughout the year.

Kevin and Kathi Zadai, you simply inspire me like you inspire the whole world. I mean, who talks about humility and serving and obedience and still fills up a conference center? Thank you for your love for the Word of God. Thank you that you simply *live* the Bible. You do the Word of God. I am blessed that I get to watch the amazing fruit bloom and blossom in your life. Thank you for letting me be the smallest part of that, because I am learning so much from you both. You are the same whether in front of a crowd or whether alone in your own room. I love you both so much and I love doing life with you.

Sid Roth, thank you for your passion for the supernatural. Thank you for your passion for the Jewish people and all that is in the heart of the Lord for them. I love praying for you. I love watching what God is doing through you. Thank you for writing this foreword and that your faith is so real and so childlike that is actually happens. What a gift you are. And what an inspiration you are to the world.

Thank you, Mark Hendrickson, for your words that flow like a river because it is who you are and how you live. You and Debbie are going to have the most amazing crowns in eternity because you stay so hidden here on the earth, yet you are so full of the likeness Jesus. It is so rare and so beautiful.

Destiny Image Publishers, thank you to everyone who has helped and believed in this book.

Tina Pugh, thank you for your encouragement, your patience, you phone calls, your texts and emails, your heart for my own words to be my words. I loved working with you.

John Martin, thank you for your patience, your kindness all through the editing process.

Thank you to the amazing editor, Tammy Fitzgerald, for this book. I loved your edits, your questions. It was a joy to work with you.

Larry Sparks, thank you for your patience in the completion of this book. Your entire staff is amazing and so encouraging. I love Destiny Image so much.

Contents

PSALMS 109:1-5

Foreword

I've interviewed Julie many times on *It's Supernatural!*, and she has become a good friend. Each time I've been struck with her pure heart and devotion to Jesus. She's a mother, wife, and anointed psalmist. She's also prophetic and just plain fun. Her early life was difficult, which was used by God to drive her to have a great hunger for more of Him. This passionate pursuit has opened up spiritual and heavenly breakthroughs with encounters that unveil heavenly treasures to us.

30 Days of Praying the Psalms is one of those fine treasures. Julie takes you on an insightful journey through the first 30 psalms. She has extracted the gold out of these psalms and lays them out like the details and clues on a treasure map.

The psalmists experienced all the attitudes and emotions that are common to us today. And even though there were some dark days, the psalmists almost always end with a "Yet will I praise You for You will save Your beloved" type confession. This confession was not only a powerful weapon of breakthrough in their day, but it is equally powerful in ours.

Julie employs real-life stories and a little self-deprecating humor to make this writing much more than just an academic workbook. She weaves her heart and soul into this book so as to make it relevant and captivating. And to put the rubber to the road, she urges the reader to implement a four-point plan with each of the passages that she highlights.

1. Pray the Word out loud.

2. Turn that Word into your prayer.

3. Write your prayers down—journal each Scripture.

4. Turn on your soaking music and sing out these choruses.

When you hear Julie sing the Psalms and pull the pathos out of the psalmists' writings, you will be hooked. Before you know it, you will find yourself singing when you didn't even think you could. You'll be inspired to try. I admit, I can't carry a tune, except when I pray in tongues—then I can carry a tune. But you know, I've found that I can follow along with Julie. So if I can do it, you can do it, too! There is such a presence of godly tranquility as she plays the piano and sings. I have felt shalom (peace), but this is almost a different level of peace. It is liquid tranquility!

I love the discovery of any new way to make Heaven's supernatural realities accessible to us. And I believe Julie Meyer has discovered a major weapon for your supernatural arsenal—a powerful weapon of breakthrough that you can use daily! God is restoring this ancient Jewish meditation method today. I can't wait for you to discover the power of praying and singing the Psalms. What an amazing way to prepare for the coming Golden Global Glory!

—Sid Roth
Host, *It's Supernatural!*

Preface

Many people pray the Psalms, memorize the Psalms, sing the Psalms, but few are walking in the benefits of the Psalms. The promises or keys written in each chapter are not only for David, but they are keys for us. For these chapters, inspired by the Holy Spirit, are for us to grab on to, reap from, and live out.

Walk with me for the next 30 days as we find keys and promises tucked away within each chapter of the Psalms. They are simple enough for every believer to walk out and will help us go from being overwhelmed with life to overcomers in life.

Where did David find the tools to craft this profound, yet eclectic, book of praise to God? The answer is that the poets' quiver is filled with his sights, senses and experiences. And specifically in *Eretz Yisrael*, where almost all of the Psalms were penned, the flora, fauna, rivers, mountains, cities, caves, kings and nations were his muse.[1]

NOTE

1. The Israel Bible, "Psalms with commentary by Rabbi Avi Baumol," Introduction, https://theisraelbible.com/bible/psalms.

Introduction

Have you ever wanted step-by-step instructions for life? Is there a way to have fulfillment and success with our children, in school, in the workplace, in our home, and with our children, and all throughout our entire lifetime? If someone could tell you how to live life with an inner fulfillment that produces outward success—would you walk out that path? We may have found the answer to all the above questions within the psalms.

Do you know that one of the *most* read books in the Bible is the Book of Psalms? We find portions of the Psalms in church services, weddings, memorials, graduations, worship services, even Presidential inaugurations—the list could go on and on. There are incredible keys written within each chapter of the Psalms that give us step-by-step instructions for life, for keeping our hearts tender, for success, for deliverance, for healing, for breakthrough, to help us deal with grief, and for repentance. There are battle plans and strategies David used in his day that we can use today, and they are wrapped within the Psalms.

The Psalms are the language of the heart. These psalms teach us how to pray when we don't know what to pray or even how to pray. When we have no language or no words, we can open the Psalms and it becomes our personal prayer to God. David wrote it but we can use these chapters to spark our own prayer life, and they will help us keep an ongoing conversation with God alive. Every single emotion known to man is found written within the chapters of this book.

From the depths of despair, sorrow, and anguish to the heights of joy, gladness, and praise—out of the longings of David's heart he wrote out his prayers and sang them back to God. Most agree that David was the author of the first book of Psalms, which starts with Psalm 1 and continues through Psalm 41. We will be looking at the first 30 chapters, so although there were several authors to the Psalms, in this book I will only be referring to David.

The Book of Psalms has brought me great comfort and has also given me the words to talk to God when I didn't know what to pray, but I have also found within each chapter simple instructions for the heart. This book reaches back in time to the very beginning with a continued mediation from the Torah and then at the same time it points us to the New Testament and beyond. In some of these chapters, David is writing about events he only saw in the spirit or a vision, which he had not actually walked out. It reads like the glue that brings the beginning and the future together. For it causes us to remember and also points us to the prophecy of future events, many of which we read in the New Testament.

The Psalms show us the pathway for encountering God. David was invited to peer into the realm of Heaven and hear *actual* conversations between the Trinity. Then he simply wrote them down and sang them out, and *we* benefit from his writings and his devotions. These psalms also reflect the inner turmoil when David felt abandoned by God. Jesus even quoted Psalm 22 as He was dying on the cross. Then David also writes about God's protection and deliverance that rescued him time and time again.

And yet what I love about David is his honesty. From his meditations on the Word of God, he put his life right in the middle of his meditations and out of that we have the Psalms. He writes about being in the depths of despair. He is discouraged, depressed, betrayed, he has no friends. He starts his prayer with raw emotions and truthfully tells God of his ongoing battles.

I believe right here lies one of David's greatest keys. Let's use the Psalms for our prayers and our meditations. Let's be *completely honest* with God as we walk out our day-by-day, step-by-step journey and as we go, learning to completely trust in God. This process is what begins to enlarge our faith, just like it did with David, so that feelings of despair and depression will *lead us* to hope and faith in God who sees all and knows all.

These Words Are Powerful

In Luke 24:44, Jesus tells His disciples, "Everything written about me in the law of Moses and the prophets and in the *Psalms must* be fulfilled" (NLT). So Luke directs us to the Psalms, showing that the Psalms point each reader straight to Jesus. In this portion of Luke, Jesus reminds His followers that everything He had told them about His life, His death, His resurrection, His kingdom was simply a fulfillment of Scripture. In fact, when reading the New Testament, the Psalms is quoted more than any other Old Testament book.

The psalms were inspired by the Spirit of the Lord. They are not just beautiful poems, but every Word is inspired by God. We find in Second Timothy 3:16:

All Scripture is inspired by God and is useful to teach us what is true and to make us realize what is wrong in our lives. It corrects us when we are wrong and teaches us to do what is right (NLT).

These psalms teach us what is true and help each one of us to realize how to make the wrong things right in our lives. They bring conviction to our lives, which *always* frees us and releases us into our God-designed destiny.

Hebrews 4:12 tells us the Word of God is alive and active; it is full of living power. When we pray these psalms aloud or sing them out, these words go forth and they begin to *create*; they begin to do what they were sent to do. They target our soul, our mind, our heart, and these words begin to transform our lives. This is the amazing power that we can witness in our own lives as we pray through the Psalms. This is the very thing that David did. He fought his battles through the Word—he would meditate on the Word and put himself in the storyline of the chapters. He fought his battles crying out to the Lord by saying the Word out loud, and then he put music to those words, to his prayers. David sang himself to victory time and time again, and I believe if it worked for David it will work for us.

Jesus fought using the same power of the Word. We see this in the Gospels. In Matthew 4, when satan tried to tempt Jesus after His forty-day fast in the wilderness, Jesus Himself fought using the Word of God by answering each temptation with "*It is written.*" Jesus overcame satan with the written Word.

How powerful is that? Can this be our battle plan? Can we fight like Jesus fought? Can we use these keys and fight like David did?

Can we take the psalms and use them to fight, to push back darkness and release His light in our everyday life? I believe we can. We have to get these words on the inside, crave the Word, think about the Word, chew this Word like a cow chews its cud, over and over and over, and pray them back to God.

My heart for this book was to not just write a sweet devotional of nice thoughts from the Psalms; I wanted to share keys, truths, directions, and instructions that are found in each chapter, showing us that if we walk and talk in these truths we will *begin* to live and walk in the benefits of the Psalms. This book will ignite our prayer life and help us to walk out a supernatural life.

These psalms give us language so that in every season we are able to keep an ongoing conversation with the Lord. Our conversation with God is ongoing and never ending, and through this continual conversation we learn how to carry our hearts before the Lord through the storms of life so that our hearts remain tender and our life in God remains strong.

One thing that helps me in my meditations and study is to unwrap some of the words in each chapter by doing a study of the Hebrew words. I love doing this because it gives me more language as I pray these psalms back to the Lord.

You may notice that in this book are comments made on both Hebrew and Greek words or phrases. Simply put, this decision was made because the psalms exist in both ancient languages, both of which were used by both Jews and Christians alike. Both languages were separately used to understand, sing, and study the psalms relevant to the time period, location, and relevant languages of the reader or listener. For example, Paul the apostle's Scriptures were a version of the Septuagint, a Greek translation of an earlier Hebrew version of the Old Testament. However, the Old Testament that most of us read is based on Hebrew texts, not Greek. Thus, because the Old Testament, and in particular the Psalms, has been treasured as Scripture in both languages, Greek and Hebrew are both sources of inspiration for this book.[1]

Additionally, when Jesus walked the earth and made references to the psalms among His disciples and those with whom He was speaking, they would have read and understood the psalms out of the Greek writings. When I read the Hebrew definitions alongside the Greek, I find they show me the same word from a different view, and it actually helps me see the word in a little different way and it gives me a greater understanding of the word within the psalm.

How to Pray Through These 30 Psalms

In starting this journey of 30 days praying the Psalms, take your time in reading through the psalm. Don't be in a hurry; think of each chapter as a luxury spa for the heart and soul. So stay in the spa a while And enjoy this refreshing spa treatment. When you read through each chapter, do your best to *not* skip ahead to your favorite psalm, because there are incredible promises in every chapter. You may want to read one chapter a week and really go deep in that psalm. The Psalms are to be felt with the heart, not just memorized but to be experienced, that our hearts would become tender as we pray through these psalms. Word by word, say them slowly; sing them, as singing slows us down a little. We want everything fast, but the Psalms were meant to be read slowly and experienced at the deepest level of our hearts.

I have four simple keys that I have used for years when praying through the Psalms each day. Maybe these will be of help to you.

Number one: Say the Word out loud. I like to picture my mouth like a fireman's hose, and when I am saying and praying these words out loud I imagine these words as strong and penetrating like the powerful blast of water that comes through the end of a fireman's hose the minute it is turned on. No man can stand if this hose is pointed in their direction. This kind of hose is used to put fires out; however, the Word of God coming out of our mouth is like the same force that will start a fire in our heart. So take each day and read the chapter, and the portion of Scripture that we are highlighting—and pray those words out loud.

Number two: Turn these couple of Scriptures into your own prayer. Put your life and your season within the passage we are praying. What are you going through? What does this season of life look like? If you are in an emotionally hard season, be honest with God and use the psalms as your words and language to bridge any gap that might be trying to hide.

Number three: Take some time and write down the psalm. There is something that makes us linger within the words of each verse when we take the time to write them out. We are not so quick to read, pray, and then move on. The action of writing each word out seems to deepen the psalm and its meaning, and at times I have felt as if I am experiencing the very same emotions that David was having when he wrote the psalm. To quote one of my heroes in the teaching of the Psalms:

Cursive handwriting quickens the brain and helps us learn and process differently. ...When we're writing scriptures by hand, deeper cognitive-processing of the words is involved which improves comprehension and memorization of the material. Think of it as an opportunity to praise the Lord in somewhat of a dance, allowing your heart to express your worship more fully as your pen dances across the silent page. Think of your pen as an instrument of praise. David's scribes were an important part of the songs in the Tabernacle of David. Had they not written the spontaneous expressions of prayers and praises and prophecies we wouldn't have them today. And remember many of the psalms were written while they were standing beside the Ark of the Covenant fully engaged in worship. An important part of their worship was the writing of His truths as they were interacting with His presence. So, it's not just about memorizing scripture it's about worship.[2]

Number four: Be really brave and sing these Scriptures out, not just softly—sing them loud. Find your own melody. There is something about singing. When we sing we use our diaphragm and all those muscles around our belly. When we take the time to sing them out, it is a fast on-ramp to get the psalms not just in our heads to memorize them—although that is good—but it is as if those words dive deep into our soul when we sing them. It is more than study; it is the difference between memorizing the psalms and actually becoming the psalms. As one of my favorite teachers said, "Don't just memorize the psalms. Be the psalms." Singing the Psalms takes you to that place.

WHAT DO YOU REMEMBER MORE — SOMETHING SOMEONE TOLD YOU YEARS AGO OR A SONG YOU SANG FROM YOUR CHILDHOOD LIKE A CHRISTMAS SONG — TRY IT.

36

In June 2016, I began to sing my way through the Psalms. Each month I began to record a new psalm. We started an online community with weekly Bible studies and monthly live interactive classes to journey together, bringing the Psalms into our everyday life. We have over 40 hours of soaking from the Psalms available on our 24/7 radio. To help you with these chapters, you may want to visit our website at intotheriver.net and download the soaking for each psalm.

Just remember, as you begin to walk through these chapters, pick up the keys found in each psalm, and put them to use—it will change your life. You can and will be the one who encourages your own heart the most by bringing these psalms into your everyday life. These psalms will empower you from the inside out. The Psalms are our battle plan for supernatural living. I have been singing the Psalms for years, but when I started at Psalm 1 in 2016 and began to sing them, record them, pray them, write them, decree them, this kept these psalms on my heart and in my mouth all my waking hours. After literally doing the very thing that I am encouraging you to do, I have found a greater passion for the Word in my heart. I cannot get enough of it. I have been reading the Psalms in this very way, so I can tell you it will set your own heart aflame for more of God and more of His Word. Then, just watch that fire spill over to everyone in your life.

So let's get started.

Pray the Word out loud.

Turn that Word into your prayer.

Write your prayers down; journal each Scripture.

Turn on your soaking and sing out these choruses.

Notes

1. Joseph Meyer studied Classical Languages and Literature at UCSB.

2. Ray Hughes, Facebook post, November 6, 2019, https://www
.facebook.com/rayhughesmusic/posts/hey-all-of-you-ready-writers-a
-few-thoughts-cursive-handwriting-quickens-the-bra/
10157936027051052.

Week 1

Day 1

David's Keys to Success

Blessed is the man who walks not in the counsel of the ungodly, nor stands in the path of sinners, nor sits in the seat of scoffers; but his delight is in the law of the Lord, and in His law he meditates day and night. He will be like a tree planted by the rivers of water, that brings forth its fruit in its season; its leaf will not wither, and whatever he does will prosper.
—Psalm 1:1-3

I walked into a local bookstore to have coffee with a friend, and as I was waiting for my grande latte with an extra shot of espresso, I began to glance at all of the books on the shelves. To my surprise, there was one word that seemed to be the subject of every book—the word *success*. There were books on success in life, in school, in raising children, success in getting into college, in staying in college, in marriage, in your job, success in weight loss, success in weight gain; there was even a book on how to have the correct mindset for success. There seemed to be every single kind of book written on having success in every area that one could think of. After scanning book after book, I thought to myself, "Has anyone read Psalm One?" Now, personally, I have never, ever, ever needed advice on successful weight gain; however, there are keys in this first chapter that will teach us how to walk through life successfully with a heart that prospers in every season, whatever our needs are for that season.

Psalm 1 shows two very different roads that lead in very different directions. It begins with the word *blessed*. Pastor David Guzik's online commentary says, "*Blessed* means supremely happy, fulfilled [with the idea of contentment]. In fact, in Hebrew the word is actually a plural, which denotes either a multiplicity, which is a large number of blessings, or an intensification of them."[1] Multiplicity can mean a wealth or a collection of blessings that are coming your way.

So how are we blessed? This is our first key: Blessed is the one who *does not* follow the counsel, the advice, or plans, of the ungodly, the guilty. For their plans come with a warning label—if we make a choice to follow their advice, soon we will be standing in their path, joining them in a multitude of wrong choices, then sitting at the table in complete fellowship with evil. Many call this road "the progression of sin." Do *not* go down this path.

This second key leads us straight onto the *correct* path: Blessed is the one who delights, the one who takes great joy and their chief passion or pleasure is searching and finding the treasures in the Word of God. Now, if you say to yourself, "Oh my gosh, the Word is not my chief delight"—that is OK. Take a deep breath, sit back, take a sip of coffee, because God loves our honesty. The amazing thing is we can turn this Scripture into prayer and ask the Holy Spirit to make the Word our chief delight, our soul's highest pleasure. He loves to answer this prayer.

The third key is *meditate* on the Word. The word *meditate* in the Hebrew has several meanings. It can mean to think about it, talk about it, to ponder, to imagine, to speak it, to sing it, to study it (Strong's

H1897). I will find the treasures of the Word a continual giving back to God and continual conversation with the Lord using His Word.

The Greek captures that a bit more. It is a fairly common verb labeled a "verb of effort." Thus, it usually has the sense of "make sure you do this!" The verb means to study, train oneself, or practice. What does it look like to study as if you are practicing an instrument or training for a competition? This is how we are to meditate on the Word of God. And we are invited to do this *at all times*.[2]

Verse 3 is our word picture. When we put to use the keys of David, we *are* this tree. We are firmly planted by rivers of water, meaning our heart and mind are alive, being fed by the Word of God. This Word becomes like fresh waters that continually give us the nourishment we need exactly when we need it. We stay fresh, we stay alive, we stay green. We do not show the signs of a dried up and dying tree, but our leaves are green and alive. The roots of this tree are getting stronger and growing deeper even in hard seasons. God's promise is that though we may not see fruit, He is bringing something good out of everything, even the hard seasons.

The outcome of using David's keys is this incredible promise. Whatever we do shall prosper. In Hebrew the word for *prosper* can mean to advance, to make progress, to succeed or be profitable, to show or experience prosperity (Strong's H6743). It can mean to finish well or one who is successful in all things. When we bring in the Greek, the verb can be translated "will be prospered" and thus invites us to carefully consider two important senses of the word. First, its force is in the future, not the present, which makes us consider *when* the effect will take place. Moreover, it's a passive verb, which means that the force of the effect is not something *you* do but what is done

PROSPER IS

GOD'S SUPERNATURAL BLESSING

to you. So one way of appreciating this verb is to think that your path in life will be good throughout its course; this is not something you can *do* but will be provided *for you*, assuming you meet the conditions of the passage.[3]

So what are the conditions? How do we step into our supernatural life full of promises? Another way to say this is, "How can our hearts stay alive and full of expectation even if we do not see motion with our eyes?" Here are our answers. Using these keys of David will keep us on the narrow road. These keys will keep us on the path of life delighting in His Word and feeding our soul on His Word, having a constant conversation with God.

Now, does this mean that we can pray for anything and receive it? Well, let's say that the keys from Psalm 1 will keep us on the right path. If we are walking on the right path, that tends to lead us to *ask God* for the right things, meaning then our prayers and requests to God will likely be aligned with His will. Jesus tells us in John 15:7: "If you remain in Me, and My words remain in you, you will ask whatever you desire, and it shall be done for you."

I want to invite you to pray aloud Psalm 1:1-3.

DAILY PRAYER

God, let me be the one who is blessed. Help me to make the right choice and choose the right path. Empower me to love Your Word so much that it is an easy choice to choose not to walk on the path listening to the schemes of the guilty and following their bad advice. Oh Lord, let my chief delight be in Your Word and help me to meditate on Your Word day and night—all the time. I will talk about it, I will study Your Word—this is my constant conversation with You. Because of this, I shall be like a tree planted beside streams of water that brings forth its fruit in its season, whose leaf does not wither, and whatever I do shall prosper or spring forth in success. I am that tree. I am walking in and using these keys of David.

Lord, I will stay on the narrow road, stay on the path of life, delighting in Your Word, meditating day and night. I will feed my soul on Your Word having continual conversation with You, God.

Day 1: Write out Psalm 1:1-3

- Pray these verses out loud.

- Listen to the soaking for Psalm 1.

- Use these verses to talk to God all day and into the night.

- Can you remember the keys from this psalm?

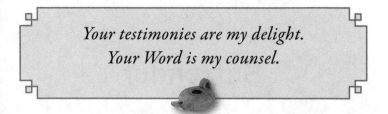

Your testimonies are my delight.
Your Word is my counsel.

Notes

1. David Guzik, "Psalm 1: The Way of the Righteous and the Way of the Ungodly," The Enduring Word Bible Commentary, https://enduringword.com/bible-commentary/psalm-1.

2. Joseph Meyer, formerly a Doctoral Fellow in Classical Languages and Literature at UCSB.

3. Joseph Meyer, formerly a Doctoral Fellow in Classical Languages and Literature at UCSB.

Day 2

Surrender

Now therefore, be wise, O kings; be instructed, you judges of the earth.
Serve the Lord with fear, and rejoice with trembling. Kiss the Son.
—Psalm 2:10-12 NKJV

This psalm reads like an unfolding four-act drama. I can almost hear music in the background, as if the intensity of the music and the shift of chords continue to build throughout each of the four scenes. Spurgeon writes, "[Psalm 2] sets forth, as in a *wondrous vision*, the tumult of the people against the Lord's anointed, the determinate purpose of God to exalt His own Son, and the ultimate reign of that Son over all his enemies."[1]

The first act would be the nations raging in defiance against God. The second act is God's response to their rage. In the third act, Jesus steps in and begins to cry aloud the promises His Father gave Him. Then in the final act, the voice of the Holy Spirit brings a charge to kings, judges, and all people on the earth.

Upon first reading this psalm, I find it fascinating that David was able to peer into the future and see this great drama unfolding. He wrote it down perfectly, as we are *right now* watching this psalm unfold and play out in the nations. David writes as if he is standing before the Trinity listening to their detailed conversation. Talk about a supernatural experience! Can you imagine having a dream or encounter in which you are right before God, His Son, and the Holy Spirit and you are listening to Their conversation?

This is the first key for Psalm 2—ask God for the same revelation and encounters to unfold in your life. What is He doing? What is He saying? We have this promise in Acts 2 of dreams and visions, so let's read Psalm 2 and ask God for more. I often ponder—what was David experiencing when writing down this psalm and hearing the anger in the nations, hearing the voice of God as He laughs at the plans of the kings? What does that even sound like? The sound of God laughing at plans to overthrow the dominion of His Son, which He has firmly set in place? Then hearing the Lord Jesus, whose voice is like the sound of many waters, declare the promises that His Father gave Him. Then, in the final act, the Holy Spirit possibly slowly turns to give a charge to the audience. He decrees His wise counsel and lays out the instructions for the kings and judges of the earth. Now if there are instructions for kings and judges, we the people are also included in this wake-up call.

Ask for more. I read Psalm 2 and the hunger for more begins to stir in my soul. I want to see God; I want to stand within the halls of eternity and just happen to walk up on a conversation between God and His Son. For in this psalm, not only does David hear a conversation, he is also shown the future. In David's day, he was waiting for a Messiah to come for the first time. There is the promise of a Savior, and David hears this intimate conversation of God telling Jesus, "Just ask Me and I will give you the nations." What do you suppose David was thinking as he was writing this whole scene down?

So I take this and the promise of Acts 2, along with the promise of John 1:51: *"Truly, truly, I say to you, you will see heaven opened, and the angels of God ascending and descending on the Son of Man"* (ESV). Lord, we want to encounter You like David did. Oh that we would hear conversations between the Godhead and then perfectly write them down and pray them out. A great Scripture to pray:

> *In the last days, God says, I will pour out my Spirit on all people. Your sons and daughters will prophesy, your young men will see visions, your old men will dream dreams. Even on my servants, both men and women, I will pour out my Spirit in those days, and they will prophesy* (Acts 2:17-18 NIV).

Our second key is to *heed the Spirit's instruction*. Can you imagine the Holy Spirit turning right to you, looking straight in your eyes, and giving instructions on how to set your heart before God as the leaders of nations are in total defiance? If Psalm 2 is calling the leaders of nations, the kings, the judges to walk out wisdom, instruction, humility, servanthood, and surrender, all while being in complete awe of God, then He is also calling us individually to the very same walk.

It has been my soul's purpose in every season to live out these last three verses. I have had to press delete, ask forgiveness, and start over many times all while signing up again. I say them to myself out loud:

> *Be wise, consider all outcomes before you act. Allow yourself to be instructed by others even if they are younger than you or know less. Serve. Love this place, don't just endure it until something better comes along. Rejoice with trembling; be in awe of the*

majesty and greatness of God. Walk out complete surrender in all things before the Lord.

Let's talk about the word *serve*. I once heard Francis Chan say, "If you show up to serve, you will never be disappointed." If we show up to be served or be the center of attention, it never works out well for that mindset. This was the whole problem with Saul when young David came onto the scene. Remember the song of the young maidens in First Samuel? As they danced, they sang: "Saul has slain his thousands, and David his tens of thousands."

When society dictates that it is most glamorous to be on top, to have the most followers on social media, Jesus does not necessarily call that serving. *Serving* means the exact opposite. Serving as Jesus taught throughout the Gospels means to bow down, be a slave to, embrace humility, be the lowest, be as a waiter doing the menial jobs. This is how we look and act like Jesus—do the jobs that you don't need any training to do. Jesus even says, "This is how you are great and you are the first."

God is working these last three verses within us right now and through our everyday lives, through our ministries, our workplaces, our relationships, our worship teams, our families, our friendships. It's His complete joy to help us be conformed more and more into the image of His Son. As we get closer and closer to the return of Jesus and the nations are raging and yelling at humanity to walk in the exact opposite way, our place is to completely surrender and allow the Holy Spirit to have His perfect work in our lives. That perfect work causes us to be like the bright and shining ones of Daniel 12:3: *"And those who are wise shall shine like the brightness of the sky above; and those who turn many to righteousness, like the stars forever and ever"* (ESV).

DAILY PRAYER

Lord, I take these words to heart and ask that You would help me to be wise, to let my heart be instructed. Help me to serve You and others in my life, letting go of all offense. Lord, I ask that You would help me to live in a holy reverence and awe of Your majestic power and greatness. Help me to boldly surrender every-thing—every dream, every plan, and every desire.

Thank You for helping me live day to day inviting Your wisdom, instruction, servanthood, and humility into my life. As I put all my trust in You, let me see and hear what David saw. I want more, Lord, in Your Name. Amen.

> *Serve and worship the awe-inspiring God. Recognize His greatness and bow before Him, trembling with reverence in His presence. Surrender, fall face down before Him, and kiss the Son.*

Psalm 1 and Psalm 2 serve as directions for living life—the foundation for reading the complete Book of Psalms. If we take up these keys, we will become unmovable, unshakeable unoffendable, and our heart will stay steady in God for years and years. As we walk through the rest of the psalms, keep the keys from Psalms 1 and 2 alive in your heart, for by using them we shall be blessed and we shall be set up for success and surrender throughout our entire life.

Day 2: Write out Psalm 2:10-12

- Pray these verses out loud.

- Listen to the soaking for Psalm 2.

- Use these verses to ask the Lord to convict and also empower you to walk in these verses.

- Can you remember the keys from this psalm?

Notes

1. Charles Spurgeon, *The Treasury of David,* "Psalm 2, Title," https://archive.spurgeon.org/treasury/treasury.php.

Day 3

Worship and Rebuttal

*But You, O Lord, are a shield for me, my glory and the
One who raises up my head.* —Psalm 3:3

It was one of David's darkest hours. The title of this psalm reveals the author and the storyline. David was fleeing from Absalom, who had started a rebellion against his father to take over the kingdom (see 2 Sam. 15–16). We find David fleeing in the dead of night with his household and those in his army whose heart was still with him. In their flight, they went out on foot, crossing the brook Kedron on the road to the wilderness. David went up the ascent of the Mount of Olives, weeping as he went. His head covered, his feet bare, followed by all those who were with him also covering their heads, their feet bare, and weeping as they went.

Second Samuel 16 tells us the storyline, but Psalm 3 shows us the innermost heart cry of a father, a husband, a priest, and a king. It is interesting that a thousand years later Jesus followed this same route (see John 18:1). "David in this was a type of the Lord Jesus Christ. He, too, fled; He, too, passed over the brook Kedron when His own people were in rebellion against Him, and with a feeble band of followers, He went to the garden of Gethsemane."[1]

Worship

As David rounded the top of the mountain, he worshiped. This act of worship, right here at this time, could be one of the many reasons God called David, "a man after My own heart." Here lies a very important key for us—*worship*. On this night, there was an urgency to flee, to get as far away from Absalom as possible, yet when David stood on the top of the mount—he worshiped. He bowed down in complete reverence to God and worshiped God there. It could have been on this very mount that the words of Psalm 3 came pouring out of David's heart. Through every emotion that he must have been struggling with, the tears, sorrow, fear, betrayal of a son, the betrayal of some of David's closest confidantes—he stopped and bowed low before the Lord. When everything was going wrong, when the promise looked as if it had failed, when the destiny seemed defeated, it was right there that David gave the Lord the honor due His name. As David would write later in Psalm 34:1, "I will bless the Lord at all times."

Let us do the same and heed this important lesson of the heart. Use this key and *always* make time for worship. When everything is perfect or when every plan fails—worship. When the hope of a promise is inches away yet suddenly falls between your fingers—worship. David was walking into the very wilderness to hide in the very place he walked out of to become king, and yet he worshiped. As the song goes, "This Is How I Fight My Battles." This is really how we fight—we pick up this key and we *worship*.

Then, as if things could not get any worse, Absalom's army was increasing. David's was decreasing. He began to sing Psalm 3. It starts with the sound of betrayal from his own son along with the betrayal of some of those closest to him. As David is fleeing, his enemies are boasting in the fact that they felt God was now done with him and unwilling to help David. They were determined to shout it out loud. "God will not help you. You deserve this fate. God has turned His back on you. God is not willing to help you anymore."

Have you ever had those feelings and thoughts of everyone being against you? Maybe you made some choices that were not wise. Maybe you totally blew it in your walk with God and people were upset with you, saying the same things, "God will not be willing to help you now." If you have ever heard these negative, hurtful words—well, hang on, because there is a sudden shift in this storyline.

David's Rebuttal

Here lies our second key—*truth*. David *refused* to believe anything that his heart and song knew to be untrue. His heart response was a declaration of truth. It was as if David was shouting forcefully the truth that was not just a hopeful thought, but truth that was alive in the depths of his heart and the deepest places of his soul. This is who he knew God to be. This is the truth. God *is my* shield.

In full confidence David replies with the steadfast truth he has walked in since his lowly shepherd days. It was something he knew deep down inside, and that knowing was rising and could not be quenched. He says, "But You, O Lord, are a *shield* for me, my glory and the One who raises up my head." He does not even address his betrayers. He turns his attention straight to the Lord.

Let's unwrap a couple of these words. Spurgeon writes of the word *shield*, "a buckler round about, a protection which shall surround a man entirely, a shield above, beneath, around, without and within."[2] In Greek this word is usually translated as "defender" or "shield." It seems to be a compound word that means "to stand against the person or thing which is trying to take me away."[3] This is a beautiful word picture of God. He stands in the gap. He stands between David and his betrayers as if to say, "I have this David."

The Word *glory* can mean honor or dignity.[4] In the Greek, since the psalm is discussing a quality of David, the simple sense of "renown" or "reputation" seems to work best. So David is reminding his betrayers; he is singing loudly to all who can hear—the Lord is my Defender. He is my renown. He is my reputation even in this situation. He is the One who lifts my head high. "There was nothing glorious or head-lifting in David's circumstances, but there was in his God."[5]

This Is Our Confidence

This is our testimony. Just like God was David's shield, He is our shield today. He surrounds us with Himself—entirely, completely, above, and beneath. He is our defender and stands against any foes or enemies or darkness that tries to creep into our lives. God stands as our constant champion defender; nothing can get by His all-powerful defense.

Use these keys—worship and truth. Worship when it's hard; worship when it's a difficult season. Then have a rebuttal to accusations and this is where we use our second key which is truth. This is what God's truth says about us. God is my wraparound shield. These are words to live by. We need to say these out loud so that they become our first response. Let's live in the reality that David lived in. He already *is*.

DAILY PRAYER

Lord, I make this confession—You are my shield. Thank You, Lord, for making me aware of the greatness of Your love. You love me so much that You give Yourself as my wraparound shield. You surround me entirely; You are above me and beneath me. Thank You that nothing can penetrate this shield. You are my reputation in every season. You are my continual defender who time and time again places Yourself between the accuser and me.

Thank You for Your great protection. Lord, I picture in my mind You as my wraparound shield. You are all around me. You all-en-circle me, entirely and completely above and beneath. Nothing can penetrate this shield. You surround me with Yourself.

Lord, as I lie down and sleep, I awake, for You sustain me. Thank You, Lord, that You keep me and You sustain me all through the watches of the night. Lord, when my troubles are so many, I lie down on Your bed of peace, Your love and kindness to me are like a heavy blanket covering me. I thank You that I have been made aware of your love, because I can feel Your love in the same way that I feel a heavy blanket covering me as I lie down and sleep.

I have One Savior, and that is You. It is why I can confidently say, "I won't be afraid."

Day 3: Write out Psalm 3

- Pray these verses out loud.

- Listen to the soaking for Psalm 3.

- Use these verses to talk to God.

- Can you remember the keys from this psalm?

NOTES

1. Spurgeon, *The Treasury of David*, "Psalm 3, Title," https://archive.spurgeon.org/treasury/treasury.php.

2. Ibid., "Psalm 3, verse 3."

3. Joseph Meyer, formerly a Doctoral Fellow in Classical Languages and Literature at UCSB.

4. Joseph Meyer: Glory δόξα is a flexible term whose context shapes its meaning. Sometimes, it is the Greek word used when translating the Hebrew הַנֶּיכָשׁ or shekinah.

5. David Guzik, "Psalm 3: Peace in the Midst of the Storm," The Enduring Word Bible Commentary, https://enduringword.com/bible-commentary/psalm-3.

Day 4

Sticks and Stones

Know that the Lord set apart the faithful for Himself;
the Lord hears when I call to Him. —Psalm 4:3

Have you ever heard the old saying, "Sticks and stones may break my bones, but words will never hurt me"? I remember learning that in grade school. It's one of those "not necessarily fun" memories. I realized something about myself—I am a "ducker." You might ask, "What is that?" Let me tell you. If I was invited to play a game that involved a ball coming directly toward my face, my first reaction was always to move out of the ball's pathway and duck.

As you can imagine, this did not make me a popular player on any team. I still have a memory of playing volleyball and watching that ball headed straight in my direction, and as I began to move out of its path I yelled, "Hers!" Well, choices like that did not make a winning team, nor did it make me especially popular with teammates.

It was not long before the words of encouragement, like, "You can catch it. We are for you. You got this," were replaced with groans of disappointment, insults, jokes—and I promise that those words *did* hurt. So the "sticks and stones" response is not even true, because

OR PEOPLE SAY WELL YOU ALREADY THOUGHT ABOUT SAYING SOMETHING HURTFULL SO GOD KNOWS ABOUT IT SO YOU MIGHT AS WELL SAY IT — NO, ASK FORGIVNESS FOR THE THOUGHT BUT, DON'T HURT SOMEONE

words hurt. We could say, "Sticks and stones may break my bones, yet words cut even deeper."

This is exactly where David found himself in Psalm 4, but magnified by a million. He was not in a game of sports but he was in the midst of sticks and stones being flung at him constantly. Many commentaries link Psalm 3 with Psalm 4, saying they most likely were written during the same timeframe. Spurgeon tells us, "The Psalm is another choice flower from the garden of affliction. Happy is it for us that David was tried, or probably we should never have heard these sweet sonnets of faith."[1]

Here, we find some of David's very own family, along with some of his closest confidantes, deserting him to join the ranks of Absalom. Their weapons of warfare were sticks and stones. They began to release an atomic bomb full of slander, lies, and accusations against David. We see this in verse two as David writes: "How long will you ruin my reputation? How long will you make groundless accusations? How long will you continue your lies?" It was as if his enemies understood that God was protecting David's physical body, so they chose a different plan. They began a war of words to emotionally wear him out and take him down. For the ruin of David's reputation also pointed to the ruin of the God whom David served, the God of Israel. These malicious words were rampant; the slander was spreading throughout the land. He was bombarded with humiliation, driving him deeper into the depths of despair as his reputation lay in ruins. David Guzik writes: "In this psalm the problem is one of malicious slander and lies. It is the psalmist's reputation rather than his person that is being attacked."[2]

This is where, we the readers, begin to watch—how is David going to respond? Is he going to speak up and defend himself? What is he going to say? For David is at one of his lowest points, yet his response to these accusations shows us that he began to remember who he was before the Lord. His response to the assassination of character was verse 3, and here lies our first key of David for Psalm 4—*set apart*. When faced with dire personal attacks on his character, he responded with, "But know that the Lord has set apart the godly for himself" (ESV).

This was his answer. It is genius. David was his own chief encourager. And not only that, he gave this psalm its title—*"To the Chief Musician. With stringed instruments. A Psalm of David"* (NIV). David put his name on this psalm and gave it to the chief musician or the choir director, as a worship song was to be sung in temple worship. To bring this into our day, we could say the chief musician is the worship leader or music director of the worship service that plans the songs.

So maybe the Lord began to remind David who he was and who chose him. What we know is David's response to lies, rumors, and slander that went all throughout his own kingdom was, "Know the Lord has set apart the godly man for Himself." He began to sing out and pray aloud, "I am that godly one. I am set apart. The Lord will answer me when I call to Him." We must pick up and use this key of David, *set apart*. When sticks and stones are thrown in our direction, this is our victorious battle plan. It does not matter if it is as small as not being able to catch a silly ball or if our kingdom is torn away. David began to build himself up in the truth that God chose him and set him apart.

This is our second key—*by God and for God*. We are invited to know, beyond a shadow of a doubt, that the Lord has set apart the godly for Himself. This is important to know. We are not chosen by just anyone. We are picked and chosen by the Creator Himself for a plan and a destiny. We are set apart for God and by God.

The word *know* means "to perceive, to understand, to find out, or to know by experience." So David responded to the slander with a perception and understanding of who he was in and before God. His song, because of all his experiences with God, became the theme of Psalm 4: "I am chosen. God chose me first." This was David's battle plan. This was his key, as if he were decreeing, "I know this. I understand that I am set apart by the hand of God."

When we search out the Greek word for "set apart," it means to "make into a marvel," like Michelangelo's sculptures or paintings—to make into a marvel or to make marvelous. So, should we find ourselves in the throes of character assassination, which in our day we see frequently all over social media, the key of David that we need to pick up and use is: "This is my battle cry. I was picked out of the crowd. I am set apart by God and set apart for God. I belong to Him because He chose me first. I am fashioned by God. This is my response to your sticks and stones. I know that I am His."

God is forming and molding us into something marvelous, like a Michelangelo masterpiece. This is our experience with God, and this experience comes from having history in God. The Lord invites us to pick up these keys of David's and use them, so our heart response to negative and vicious attacks on our reputation is: "I am set apart for God. I am His artistic work in progress, and through this He is forming beauty and strength on the inside so that I will look like a Michelangelo sculpture or painting."

So pick up these keys and use them. Do not get caught up in the chaos when sticks and stones are hurled from all sides. Let's pick up these keys of David and get caught up in who we are before God. God says we are as a Michelangelo painting or sculpture. We are picked and chosen out of a crowd to fulfill the purposes that God created for us to walk in.

DAILY PRAYER

Lord, this is my prayer of thankfulness to You—that in the same way You were a support and help to David, You will be the same for me. When the battle of sticks and stones arises, when hurtful words, rumors, and slander come from every side, You will help me to remember to pray. "You have set apart the godly one for Yourself. You hear my prayers." Thank You for Your help, Lord, You teach me to use the very same key that David used. This will be my confidence as I say out loud, "I am Your masterpiece. I am set apart for you." You always hear my cry when I lift my voice. Lord, You are helping me even now to know: I have been set apart by God, set apart for God; I am Yours. Thank You, Lord.

You picked me out of the crowd. You fashioned me. I can say that I am fashioned by God. I will keep that my focus. You are the righteous God who is so merciful to me. For You alone make me dwell in safety.

Day 4: Write out Psalm 4

- Pray these verses out loud.
- Listen to the soaking for Psalm 4.
- Use these verses to talk to God.
- Can you remember the keys from this psalm?

> *You took me out of the crowd—fashioned by God, set apart for God, set apart by God. I'm Yours.*

NOTES

1. Charles Spurgeon, *The Treasury of David*, "Psalm 4, Division," https://archive.spurgeon.org/treasury/treasury.php.
2. David Guzik, "Psalm 4: Talking to God and Men," The Enduring Word Bible Commentary, https://enduringword.com/bible-commentary/psalm-4.

Morning Expectations

Give ear to my words, O Lord; consider my meditation. Listen to the
voice of my cry, my King and my God, for to You will I pray.
O Lord, in the morning You will hear my voice; in the morning
I will direct my prayer to You, and I will watch expectantly.
—Psalm 5:1-3

The very first Scripture I remember singing was Psalm 5. In fact, when I learned this song I did not realize at the time that it was word-for-word Scripture. However, this psalm has stayed with me throughout the decades. It is still one of my favorite choruses to pull out in worship. And it reminds me how easy it is to simply talk to the Lord.

So here we are again, David surrounded by endless rumors and lies, yet the tenderness of the opening verses show someone who might have kept the keys of Psalm 4 in his hand and in his heart as he began to lift up this prayer before the Lord. These keys build upon each other. David, very possibly, was encouraging himself, "I am set apart by God, I am set apart for God." Therefore, he penned this intimate psalm.

Now, I have personally never been a morning person. So there is much grace to anyone who loves to pray and study in the evening hours. I understand the great conflict of early morning hours if you happen to be a night owl. I understand if you need a pot of coffee before you are coherent enough to have a conversation with another human—I get that, but you can still benefit from this first key.

The first key is three words in the second line—*in the morning*. David actually repeats those same three words in his next sentence as if to really drive the point home. These three words are crucial—*in the morning*. In the early morning hours, when our eyelids first open to see the sun's rays peeking through the skies, we need to ask the Lord to give us an awareness that God *is* already attentive to our prayer. God is already bending down to hear our voice. He is already listening. We need this awareness that we have His attentive ear. He has been waiting all night for us to wake up. He is available, and He is waiting with excitement to hear the sound of our voice.

We can have our devotions at night. We can have our study time at night; we can do our Scripture memory in the evening hours; but we are greatly missing this important key and an amazing relationship with the Father if we wake up with no awareness that He is already listening and He is already waiting just to hear the sound of our voice. The minute I wake up, I picture God right there, already bending down to listen to my cry and prayer.

So when the dawn shines forth with its brilliant rays through the clouds—God is already waiting to hear the sound of you.

When I first began to sing Psalm 5 every day, I would study it at night, pray it out loud. However, an amazing thing began to happen in the early morning hours. I found myself waking up before the sun, and, miraculously, I was in a *good mood* before a cup of joe. My first thought was *not* of coffee. When I began to sing, pray, write down, and decree Psalm 5, my body actually responded to this prayer, and I began to wake up before the sunrise, without an alarm clock—without a thought of coffee. *This* is a miracle—just ask my husband!

As I began to pray Psalm 5, I would wake up and my first thought was, "God, You are already waiting for me to wake up. Here I am, Lord." This was quite miraculous. As my body would wake up, my eyes would open and my whole being was attentive to the Lord. My first thoughts in the early morning hours were of God. "Lord, You are already here. You are already listening to my voice."

From my experience, if you want to become a morning person and get up early to have your prayer time and your study time—just pray through Psalm 5 for a month. Because it will surely happen to you in the same way it happened to me. Your body will respond to the prayers that you are praying from this psalm. And if you include those three little words, *in the morning*, I promise you that your schedule will change abruptly, as this is the power of the Word of God. When it gets on the inside of you, it begins to work and bring the dead and dormant things alive. It begins to say, "Wake up. Wake up."

This brings us to our second key for Psalm 5. The second key in this beautiful psalm is the word *direct*. When we arise in the morning knowing that the Lord is already attentive to us, understanding His availability, Psalm 5 reminds us to *direct our prayers* to the Lord. This word can mean "to arrange, to set out, or to lay in order" as in, "to set in place or to put in a row." We lay our prayers out in order, one by one, before the Father knowing that He will not forget even the smallest cry.

I think of David in the desert. If you know anything about the desert—it's hot. It's dangerous, with poisonous snakes, scorpions, wild animals. We know this, as David writes that he killed a lion and a bear protecting his few sheep. There was a deep need to trust God for food, water, and shade. And this was the training ground for David as a shepherd. I have been to the back hills of Bethlehem, and it is dirt and sand and desert for miles and miles. This is how he learned to worship and how he learned that God really does hear his tiny cry. God led him to the places he needed for shade, food, water; and he also experienced God hearing his prayers, his songs; and he understood that God not only listens, but that God answers when prayers are laid out and directed to Him.

The third key for Psalm 5 is the word *expectantly*. How many times have you gone about your day, praying through prayer lists, but you forget to watch for the answer? Our prayer lists get longer and longer, and the business of life can keep us from taking the time to write down our requests and to *expectantly* watch for the answers to come to every prayer request.

So we have prayed Psalm 5. We suddenly find ourselves awake in the early morning hours and aware that God has bent His ear to hear our cries. We lift our prayers before the Lord and we lay them out, one by one, as if to not forget even the smallest prayer. Then we *expectantly* wait for the answer. With every prayer there must be an expectancy, an eager gaze that God is answering.

So when we lift up our prayers, we have a responsibility to pray them through until we see the answer. We lay out our prayers one by one and then watch as if at any moment in time the answer is going to fall through the roof. We watch and wait with an expectant hope that at any second the answer to our cries will come rushing through our front door. These are three very important keys that will change our life if we will use them.

DAILY PRAYER

In the morning when I rise, before the dawn breaks, before the sun's rays, the first cry You'll hear is mine.

O Lord, hear my prayers. Consider my meditations. Listen to the sound of my voice. You are my King. You are my God. I will pray to You. I will lift my voice the first thing in the morning. Oh Lord, before the sun, when the grass still shines with the morning dew, You will hear my voice.

Lord. When You wake me before the dawn breaks, let my first thoughts be of You. Let my first words be to You. You are already attentive to my cries. You are already longing to answer my prayers. Thank You, Lord, for giving me an awareness of the nearness of You as I awake to thoughts about my kind Father. I will watch and wait with eagerness for how You will answer. I will be looking up. I will be watching all throughout the day for Your kind answer. Each morning, I will set my prayers in order and lay them out before You and eagerly watch for the answer, for surely the answer will come. Thank You, Lord. Amen.

Day 5: Write out Psalm 5

- Pray these verses out loud.

- Listen to the soaking for Psalm 5.

- Use these verses to pray, to write out your prayer, and expectantly watch for the answers to come.

- Can you remember the keys from this psalm?

Before the birds begin to sing and when the grass is wet with dew and as the moon shines bright and free, You will hear from me, God.

Day 6

The Voice of Weeping

Be gracious to me, O Lord, for I am weak; O Lord, heal me. ...The
Lord has heard the voice of my weeping. —Psalm 6:2,8

Have you ever gone through a period of time when the circumstances you were walking through were so heart wrenching and so heartbreaking that when you sat down to pray there were no words to say, there were only countless tears that seemed to fall to the ground? Maybe there was a season when you couldn't find your words and all you had were tears. This is where we find David in Psalm 6, and we can tell from the first seven verses that his grief, his pain, and his tears were unbearable. I love what Spurgeon says about this psalm: "Weeping is the eloquence of sorrow. It is an unstammering orator, needing no interpreter, but understood of all. Is it not sweet to believe that our tears are understood even when words fail? Let us learn to think of tears as liquid prayers, and of weeping as a constant dropping of importunate intercession which will wear its way right surely into the very heart of mercy."[1]

When circumstances in life seem to meet us at every turn with heartache and when we have no words, this is our key for Psalm 6. *Our tears count.* Our tears have a voice. I have no words to pray, but

I have a multitude of tears that continue to fall. And David shows us in this psalm that our tears actually have a sound in Heaven as David calls these tears the "voice of weeping."

This psalm could be called a psalm of sorrow or a psalm of repentance. It is the first of seven psalms of confession or sorrow. We don't know exactly what David was going through, but some commentaries have tagged this psalm in the same season as Psalms 3 through 5. David finds himself in a deep season of grief. He is aware of his weakness and the sin in his life, and it has brought him to a place of great mourning. The very simple plea in the second Scripture of this psalm is all the prayer we need: "*Be gracious to me, O Lord, for I am weak; O Lord, heal me.*" If you can take this one portion of Scripture and tuck it away in your heart, it is a comforting prayer in trying and difficult times.

This psalm starts out with David crying out for God to not discipline him in His hot displeasure. Now, I do not believe that when we come to the Lord asking for mercy He has hot displeasure over our lives. David is writing Psalm 6 out of the lens of the Old Covenant, and as we pray and sing through this psalm we have the New Covenant—we have the knowledge that Jesus took our place. All of our sin and failure was laid upon Him, and that hot displeasure from God went upon Him—therefore, God views us through the blood of His Son.

We are adopted into the family of God. We are true sons and daughters. What we can gain from Psalm 6 is that just as our earthly father will discipline his children because he loves them, so will God discipline us, but it's through the eyes of love because the price has already been paid and the sacrifice has already been given. This is the spirit of adoption. We do not walk in the hot displeasure of God. We do not walk in condemnation, as Paul writes in Romans 8:1,15:

> *There is therefore now no condemnation for those who are in Messiah Yeshua, who walk not according to the flesh, but according to the Spirit. ...For you have not received the spirit of slavery again to fear. But you have received the Spirit of adoption, by whom we cry, "Abba, Father"* (TSB).

We are adopted into God's big, beautiful family. We are sons and daughters, and He disciplines and He corrects those He loves. This is the way we want to pray through Psalm 6, for the spirit of adoption is at work in our lives.

David's cry for mercy is a groan, a deep moaning. If you have ever been in the depths of despair so deep that when you pray, there are no words, you find your voice sounding like a deep moan—this is the heart wrenching plea of David. He says, "Heal me, oh God, for my bones are troubled." It is as if he is saying, "I can feel this agony deep in my bones." He is talking about his body being weak, and he feels it clear down into the inner marrow of his bones as he cries out for God to heal him.

Can you picture in your mind someone in grief to the point of only hearing inner groanings? He writes that every single thing inside—his emotions, his thoughts, clear down to his bones—is crying out for healing, "I am in agony and I am asking for mercy." He writes that he is crying all day long and all night long and that his tears have become his food as he continues to lift up his pleas for mercy. Sometimes life is a struggle, and we wrestle with things we never expected to cross our path. We can struggle to understand death, loss, sickness, unanswered questions, and prayers that seem to continue without a quick answer or remedy; and all we can do is cry.

I have sat with friends throughout life who have walked through the loss of a spouse, a child, or a marriage, where questions prevail that may not get answered on this side of time. In those seasons when words were not enough, the only thing we did together was sit silently and cry together. We will not always have an answer—sometimes we won't understand until we step into eternity—but Psalm 6 gives us permission to weep, to feel the depths of pain, to cry as we feel the agony of brokenness. Yet at the same time, David writes in verse 8 that our tears have a sound. He writes, "The Lord has heard the voice of my weeping." This is the key in Psalm 6—*those tears have a voice*. They have a sound that God hears. The voice of weeping is a real cry and a real prayer. Use this key when you have no words to say. It works and God answers.

Have you ever pondered this? That tears have a sound? They sound like something in the realm of eternity. Tears have a voice even though someone may not ever speak words. When we unwrap this word, *voice*, in the Hebrew it can mean "noise, sound, like the sound of an instrument." Our tears are like an instrument making a sound that God hears, that God is attentive to. In the Greek it literally reads "sound of my weeping." The Lord has heard the *sound of my weeping*.

We will all face those times and those days when all we know to do is cry. Those tears are beautiful to God—Psalm 56 tells us that God keeps all of our tears in His bottle. Not one tear is wasted, and not one tear is unseen or forgotten. They are caught in His bottle, captured for the viewing of God Himself, revealing our hearts' affections for God when we are not capable of words, only the droplets of tears. Pastor David Guzik writes: "Weeping has a voice before God. It isn't that God is impressed by emotional displays, but a passionate heart impresses Him. David wasn't afraid to cry before the Lord, and God honored the voice of his weeping."[2]

This is a very important key—*those tears have a voice.* We should never ever let go of this key all throughout our life. Our tears have a sound; they have a voice. God hears the voice of our tears sometimes better than the voice of our words. "Weeping hath a voice, and as music upon the water sounds farther and more harmoniously than upon the land, so prayers, joined with tears, cry louder in God's ears, and make sweeter music than when tears are absent."[3]

DAILY PRAYER

Lord, heal me for I am so weak. Have mercy on me for I am in need. I need You, God. When my voice was silent, when I had no words, You still understood and heard the voice of my tears. I will remind myself that You, Lord, have seen every tear fall. You have listened and been attentive to my deepest groans inside. You, oh Lord, are my Healer, and I am strengthened in this—You are not just the God of David; You are my God.

I pray that I would be strengthened with divine might in my inner man as I pray through Psalm 6. Help me realize and understand that You hear every single prayer, even when the sound of my prayer is weeping, for even my tears have a voice before You. Let Your wraparound presence come and rescue me.

Save me, oh God, because of Your never-ending kindness and mercy. In Your Name, amen.

Day 6: Write out Psalm 6

- Pray these verses out loud.
- Listen to the soaking for Psalm 6.
- Use these verses to talk to God.
- Can you remember the keys from this psalm?

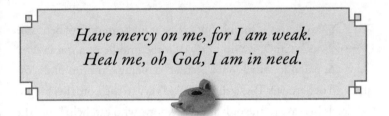

Have mercy on me, for I am weak.
Heal me, oh God, I am in need.

NOTES

1. Charles Spurgeon, *The Treasury of David*, "Psalm 6, verse 8," https://archive.spurgeon.org/treasury/treasury.php.

2. David Guzik, "Psalm 6: A Confident Answer to an Agonized Plea," The Enduring Word Bible Commentary, https://enduringword.com/bible-commentary/psalm-6.

3. Spurgeon, *The Treasury of David*, "Psalm 6, verse 8."

Song of the Slandered Saint

God, your wraparound presence is my protection and my defense. You bring victory to all who reach out for you. —Psalm 7:10 TPT

Have you ever found yourself right in the middle of betrayal? In Psalm 7, we find David in the middle of a smear campaign in which he is accused of being a traitor, of disloyalty, and of betrayal. This psalm is David's cry to the Lord, his song as he pleads his case to the only One he knows who can help him. The psalm starts with a plea and ends in a triumphant song of praise to the Most High, who makes everything alright in the end. Spurgeon writes, "What a blessing it would be if we could turn even the most disastrous event into a theme for song, and so turn the tables upon our great enemy."[1] This is exactly what David did in Psalm 7. He took a disastrous event and turned it to a theme song of praise, and the enemy crumbled.

If you have ever been in the middle of a storm of slander, these winds can pick up out of nowhere and turn a small dust cloud into a typhoon of grief, lies, and rumors that seem to build every time they are shared. David had an important key that will help us find our footing as we navigate through these treacherous waters. He shows us in Psalm 7 how to walk in confidence with a heart secured on a victory though the battle was still being fought. When the storm was raging the strongest, David saw victory in the distance and began pulling on the heartstrings of the Almighty.

He wasted no time before he began his plea. This is our key—*let God defend our cause.* David did not try to defend his cause before people. He did not direct his words to people or his enemies. He looked a little higher and cried out for God to defend him. He pleaded with God alone to speak on his behalf. He did not come out to fight the battle with great words of wisdom; he did not bring witnesses who could testify on his behalf. He came out calling on God, declaring in song that he had turned aside and hid himself in God.

The King James Version says, "*O Lord my God, in thee do I put my trust: save me from all them that persecute me, and deliver me*" (Ps. 7:1 KJV). Wrapped up in that one little word, *trust,* is the need and promise for refuge and protection that only God can give. He is writing, "I am trusting in You, God; as I turn, as I flee and seek refuge, You are my sole protection."

David reminds God of the very real danger that is lurking around him. In verse 2 he compares his enemies and their lying words to a lion that is waiting to tear his soul and rend it in pieces. Now remember, David had already fought the lion and the bear. We see this in First Samuel 17:34-35:

> When a lion or a bear came and took a lamb from the
> flock, I went out after him and attacked him, and rescued

it from his mouth; and when he rose up against me, I
seized him by his beard and struck him and killed him
(NASB).

So David had a firsthand visual of the violent attack of a lion when it is going after its prey. He had already conquered the lion and rescued the lamb from its clenching jaws. In this psalm, it is almost as if David is asking God to do for him just as David had done for the sheep he tended. David understood more than anyone that this was the duty and job of the shepherd. So he makes this comparison, saying that his enemies want to tear his soul to pieces just like the jaws of a lion rending his soul to shreds, and he calls upon God to be his refuge and place of safety, just as David was a refuge and place of safety to each lamb he tended. This is such an important key in life— *let God defend our cause.* We need to pick up this key that David used and direct all of our cries to God to defend us. We can cry out to God to direct our pleas and prayers instead of fighting an endless battle of words with people. David did not use his words in a fight with his enemies—he went beyond people. He went to the top.

If we would do as David did and use this key, looking and trusting only in the deliverance of God, we would win way more battles. David did not give a second thought to responding to his enemies on their level, with a war of words. He went straight to the top. He went straight to God and asked God to defend his actions.

In verse 8 he then writes, *"You are the Exalted One who judges the people, so vindicate me publicly and restore my honor and integrity. Before all the people declare me innocent"* (TPT). David makes this cry to God for public vindication and restoration of his honor.

Again, he is not looking to man for this. He looks up. He looks higher and sings out of his own storyline, remembering his own days as a lowly shepherd guarding his own sheep.

What a word picture. I picture in my mind David, hearing all of these rumors and slanderous lies, and he remembers his own story when he was the protector and when he was the shepherd. So David makes this choice to turn—he turns aside. He turns to God. He calls upon God an unrelenting plea for public restoration. David does not want to be his own defense; he wants God to show Himself strong on David's behalf and he wants everyone to see God standing up for David.

Rumors and slander happened many times in his life, but he gave us this amazing equipping key. David did not just say, "Make this disaster go away." He welcomed the fight and said, "God, stand up in a way that every enemy will see that You are standing up for me. God, publicly declare my innocence and vindicate my honor and integrity." Keep this key close—*let God defend our cause.*

"David knew he was at a significant disadvantage before his enemies and had to rely on the defense that is of God."[2] He writes in verse 10 that God is his defense. It is as if he actually sees God as a shield that is wrapped all around himself. God holds my shield and protects me with a shield. I look for defense and safety in no other; my hope for shelter in a time of danger is placed in God alone.

Can you picture in your mind this shield that God is holding to defend you just like he did with David? It is a shield that goes all the way around you, it covers you entirely and completely. This shield is also above and beneath you, for He wraps you in Himself. He puts you in the middle of His presence so that you are untouchable.

Can we trust Him enough to turn aside from all of the chaos and turn to God with all we are and let God be our great defender just like he was to David? This was a key that David used all throughout his lifetime—*let God defend our cause.* It kept him in the place of leaning on God alone and looking to God for answers, for deliverance, and for victory. We can pick up this same key when fighting similar battles. God is our defense—He is our wraparound presence. He is our protection and defense. He brings victory to all who reach out for His help.

DAILY PRAYER

Lord, I thank You for Psalm 7—I thank You that You have given me an equipping key, which is to turn aside and hide my soul in You. Help me to lean upon You as my defense—help me to turn to You. Help me to trust that You are my great defender. I love the confidence that David had in You; oh Lord, let that confidence be found in me. Oh Lord, in You I take refuge—save and deliver me. It's my cry to You, my plea for help. It's my song to You, for no one else can save me. Oh Lord, my God, I turn aside to hide my soul in You. Save and deliver me from those who pursue me with slander and words untrue. Reward and prosper the cause of the righteous for You are the righteous God, searching the soul, looking deep in the heart to examine the motives and thoughts.

Arise, O Lord, and stand up for Me. You wrap Your presence all around me. It's my protection—Your presence. It's all around me—my unseen protection from God. I'm untouchable in the middle of Your presence. I will trust in You.

Day 7: Write out Psalm 7

- Pray these verses out loud.
- Listen to the soaking for Psalm 7.
- Use these verses to talk to God.
- Can you remember the keys from this psalm?

> *You wrap Your presence all around me.*
> *My unseen protection is God.*

NOTES

1. Charles Spurgeon, *The Treasury of David*, "Psalm 7, Title," https://archive.spurgeon.org/treasury/treasury.php.

2. David Guzik, "Psalm 7: Confidence in God's Deliverance," The Enduring Word Bible Commentary, https://enduringword.com/bible-commentary/psalm-7.

Week 2

Day 8

Consider

*When I consider Your heavens, the work of Your fingers, the moon
and the stars, which You have established, what is man that You are
mindful of him, and the son of man that You attend to him? For You
have made him a little lower than the angels, and crowned him with
glory and honor. You have given him dominion over the works of Your
hands; You have put all things under his feet.* —Psalm 8:3-6

Have you ever gazed at the mere beauty and power of creation and wondered how God could ever put it together
and continue to hold it together? Have you ever looked
and watched as each star appears and begins its dance across the sky,
shimmering in the darkness of the night? Have you ever, when looking upon the beauty and majesty of the heavens, asked yourself the
question that David asked? "What is man that You are mindful of
him?"

In Psalm 8, David looks at the heavens and sees the majesty and
power of God and suddenly creation itself is David's classroom. He
very well could have been reciting and singing out his meditations,
which could have been from Genesis 1: "*In the beginning God created
the heavens and the earth,*" for we find a lot of Genesis 1 in this psalm.

Psalm 8 reveals David as he is beholding the God of creation and singing out his own storyline as he *considers* the heavens.

In *The Treasury of David* commentary, Spurgeon writes, "We may style this Psalm the Song of the Astronomer: let us go abroad and sing it beneath the starry heavens at eventide, for it is very probable that in such a position, it first occurred to the poet's mind."[1]

On my first invitation to Israel, I wanted to see Bethlehem and to look upon those back hills. I wanted to see the place where he sang his many meditations and wrote his many psalms. I wanted to walk on those very back hills and feel the ground beneath my feet. Those very back hills where he was in the gaze of God. This necessary time frame in David's life would lead to God taking him "from the sheep-fold, from following the sheep," and making David ruler over God's people and over Israel.

Now during the day, this was a hot, desert place; however, when evening would set in and the cool of the night breeze would begin to flow, the stars would begin their song in the night and come out one by one. These stars in the sky seemed infinite, going on for miles and miles.

Can *you* take a minute and picture David on the back hills of Bethlehem as a young shepherd boy tending his sheep? He looks up into the night sky and his thoughts become his song to God. Maybe right there, he begins to write his meditations and sing out his prayers, with no one listening but the few sheep still awake.

Here is where I ponder, and my pondering leads me to a key. The key is—*consider*. David looks at the heavens he says, "When I *consider* the heavens." This is a very important key because it requires our time, awareness, personal observation, and investment. Using this key is not a mere suggestion, and it cannot or must not be used when one is in a hurry. David is looking and observing. He is looking with a purpose, and right here I believe he begins to see more. Looking straight up into the starry host, he sees himself.

I can almost see, in my ponderings, a wind of revelation suddenly striking his heart, and his response is an explosion in song. He shouts and proclaims in the midst of his study of the night sky, "Who is man that You are mindful of him? God, You even think about me. Who is the son of man that You visit him?" I can even hear the echo of his voice as it continues over the hills and through the ravines. It started when David used this important key—*consider*. It is like all his observations have now become his answer. He realizes that the same fingers that formed and fashioned the heavens and the stars were the same fingers that formed and fashioned David. He has a realization that he was God's handiwork in the same way that the beauty and glory of the heavens were God's handiwork. I love the Greek meaning for this word *mindful*, it means "to inspect" like a general who confirms the readiness of his army.[2] It is like divine communication that starts with this key—*consider*. We pick up this key, we use it, we consider, and God answers back with, "I am making you ready. I am gladly inspecting you from your innermost parts so you are ready to step into all that I created you to be."

This is a picture of God as the Master Potter who is forming the most beautiful vessel. And the Potter steps back over and over and inspects and smooths out rough edges. The Potter continues this inspection and examination until this vessel is stunning, beautiful, and flawless from the inside to the outside.

I believe this is what God did in David's life, and this is what God does in our life. This process will happen over and over, all the while making us shine brighter and brighter. It is the joy of an ever-learning walk with the reality that God is for us, working in us, and that work will cause us to shine. It empowers us to believe and embrace who we were created to be at the very beginning, written down in Genesis 1 and sung by David in Psalm 8. God's desire is to reveal Himself and His glory through man. He desires for us to embrace that we are created in His image, living on the earth as His image bearers, walking in confidence that He has given all things under our feet.

I can honestly say as I was writing and praying through this chapter—I almost feel as if God, who is outside of time, picked me up and took me back to this time in David's life, giving me just a glimpse of the unfolding of Psalm 8. I feel as if in praying and singing through this psalm God invited me into the very emotions of David as revelation broke through and I could see in my ponderings as David stepped into his identity before God.

This one key, *consider*, leads David to see himself right at the beginning in Genesis 1, created in the image of God with all things under his feet. This very same invitation is also ours. Let's start by using this key—*consider.*

> *Then God said, "Let us make man in our image, after our likeness, and let them have dominion over the fish of the sea, and over the birds of the air, and over the livestock, and over all the earth, and over every creeping thing that creeps on the earth."*

So God created man in His own image; in the image of
God He created him; male and female He created them.
God blessed them and said to them, "Be fruitful and mul-
tiply, and replenish the earth and subdue it. Rule over the
fish of the sea and over the birds of the air and over every
living thing that moves on the earth" (Genesis 1:26-28).

This is God's reality about us. He thinks about us. He enjoys us. He is involved in our lives. He pauses to look upon our concerns. God is great and He is personal. He sees you and me in the same light and beauty that we see when we look at the heavens. This was David's classroom, and it will be our classroom. We are God's handiwork. Paul says it another way in Ephesians 2:10: *"For we are His work-*
manship, created in Christ Jesus for good works, which God prepared
beforehand, so that we should walk in them."

Let me encourage you to pray this prayer out loud as the sun is going down and the stars begin to peek through the night sky. Let's ask the Lord to open wide the doors for encounter, just like He did with David as David began to *consider*. Let's use this key too.

DAILY PRAYER

Lord, I believe that just by saying these words and singing them
out, You will reveal Yourself to me in the same way You revealed
Yourself to David. I also proclaim that Your name is wonderful.
Your name is great. Your name is excellent in all the earth and
in every single place.

Lord, let me pick up this key, consider, and use it every single evening as I look at the night sky. Let my eyes see all of the beauty that You put in place for man. Let Your majesty stream down from the heavens, filling up the earth with the fame of Your name. Let Your beauty shining in the heavens fill everywhere with the fame of Your name, with the beauty of Your name, and let it be seen in every place. Thank You, Lord, for such beauty.

When I look up at the sky, when I look up at the stars, when I look at the beauty of creation, show me who I am before You. Let me slow down and spend time considering all that You created and made with Your fingers. Show me that in all my ways, You are thinking about me, and You have me on Your mind. Let me remember through every season I am on Your mind—I am in Your heart.

Oh Lord, let me take the time to consider that the same way that I look at the beauty of the stars and feel in awe of the greatness of who You are, that You also look at me the very same way. You are in awe of what You have created within me. Help me to encounter You like David, and speak into my soul who You say I am.

Day 8: Write out Psalm 8

- Pray these verses out loud.
- Listen to the soaking for Psalm 8.
- Use these verses to talk to God.
- Can you remember the keys from this psalm?

> *The creator of it all is God. The lover of my heart is God. And the One who fashioned me is God.*

NOTES

1. Charles Spurgeon, *The Treasury of David*, "Psalm 8, Title," https://archive.spurgeon.org/treasury/treasury.php.

2. Joseph Meyer, formerly a Doctoral Fellow in Classical Languages and Literature at UCSB.

Day 9

Praise and a Whole Heart

I will give thanks to You, O Lord, with my whole heart;
I will declare all Your marvelous works.
—Psalm 9:1

May everyone who knows your mercy keep putting their trust in you.
—Psalm 9:10 TPT

Have you ever sat down to ponder the many marvelous works that God has done in your life? The testimonies of the kindness of God, who was always there to bring victory. Well, can you picture David somewhere in the decade of his 60s as he begins to write Psalm 9? Many believe that David wrote Psalm 9 in his later years, possibly remembering some of the marvelous works of the Lord that David got to be a part of. In David Guzik's commentary, he writes:

Some...apply that title as the ancient Chaldee version does: "Concerning the death of the Champion who went out between the camps," referring to Goliath. Perhaps David wrote this psalm remembering the victory over Goliath from the vantage point of many years since that triumph.[1]

So we find David, many years after the fall of Goliath, pondering and remembering this great victory. I picture David praying these words and looking out during the evening hours at the very stars he wrote about in Psalm 8. Or maybe it was the cool of the morning and he was looking out upon creation as the sun's rays began to peek through the clouds, and he remembered the day that God showed His wonderful deeds through the fall of a Philistine giant. This was no small victory, for Goliath was nine feet and nine inches. He had armor and weapons to match his size. Every day he came out taunting the armies of Israel, saying, "I am the Philistine champion, but you are only the servants of Saul. Choose one man to come down here and fight me!"

And they did choose; that day the giant fell because of one smooth stone in the hands of a young shepherd boy whose sole confidence was in his God. With that memory possibly replaying in David's mind, I can picture him as he picks up his pen, thinking of the great victory that took him from the pastures to the palace. He begins to pen a song of celebration for the many victories and the unceasing faithfulness of God. As he was looking back over his life, maybe he wanted to write down this victory and triumph for all future generations, keeping a record for each one to pass on and tell of the wonderful works of God.

The very memory of this victory causes David to burst out with praise as he writes down his prayer: "I will praise You." Then, in the same breath, he shows us that this is not mere lip service, it is not just a nice song, but after all the years and the decades that David has lived we find him still full of passion and fire. He is still praising the Lord with his heart still burning as he writes "with my whole heart." This is not a half-hearted thank you; after the highs and the lows of his life, he still writes, "I will praise You alone, Lord, with all that I am and all that is within me. I have set my whole self, my whole being to praise You, Lord." This is an important truth for us to embrace, and here lies our first key from Psalm 9—*I will praise.* To use this key is to pray these very same words—*I will praise You, O Lord.*

It is an honor that we get to praise the Lord, to worship Him with our life. The word *praise* can mean to give thanks, to be thankful; it can mean to revere or worship (with extended hands). It is as if this memory causes David so much joy, gratitude, and delight that even decades later, he continues his worship to God for the victory. We have this word picture of exuberant praise with arms lifted and hands reaching upward toward the heavens and David shouting, "I will praise You, O Lord."

This key, *I will praise,* we need to keep close and use it every single day. You can literally just camp out here to pray and sing this Scripture over and over to the Lord. The more we praise the Lord for His goodness, the more thankful we become for all that He has done.

Thankfulness within the human heart needs to be cultivated, meaning it is not a natural emotion that flows out or springs out of the human heart. We have to cultivate thankfulness and praise to the Lord by telling Him over and over, "*I will praise. I will thanks to You. I will praise You alone.*" You can never pray this too many times. The more we pray these words to the Lord, it is as if we are working that inward muscle called thankfulness and praise to the Lord until there is no landing place at all in the depths of the heart and soul for any offense. Here is our key: "I will praise. I will praise You, O Lord. I will thank You." This key will do a work on the innermost part of each of us so that we are all shining with a heart of thankfulness that overflows in praise to the Lord. This key is the one we need that will keep us steady in God with a thankful heart throughout all of life's journey.

There is another key in this psalm; it is *whole heart*. David writes that he will not give to the Lord half-hearted praise, but he will praise the Lord with his *whole heart*. This can mean "with my mind, my will, my understanding." It can be our knowledge, our soul, and our conscience. Our whole heart involves our passions, our appetites, our emotions. This key called *whole heart* keeps every part of our body involved in praising the Lord and lifting a thankful heart. It calls everything within us into this divine act of praise. Imagine all of our passions and emotions and thoughts arising in thankfulness as *everything* within us says, "*I will praise the Lord continually with all of my being.*" These two keys will change our entire prayer life.

What giants are you fighting in your life? Boldness and confidence to take down any giant begins with this first key—*I will praise*—and it continues with the second key, with how we praise, which is *with our whole heart*. Oh Lord, with every breath and thought, with every word on my lips, I will praise You. I believe that Psalm 9 reveals that the same God who delivered Israel and gave David the victory that day is the same God with the very same power, strength, and might, and He steps into our lives today. He steps in with His greatness, His might, His desire to deliver and save and help each of us as we call on Him. We may be facing such big giants before us and all we hold in our hands is a slingshot and a smooth rock, but we have to look at who is standing with us and fighting alongside us. Psalm 9 reveals the faithfulness of God all throughout David's life. If this was true for David, it most certainly is true for you and me.

Now the outcome of using these two keys is that we will begin to see and understand His mercy in a whole new way. For our whole body, soul, and spirit is now aligned in praising Him. Therefore, we will also begin to trust in the Lord in completely new ways. Our trust barometer will be off the charts. This happens as a result of new revelations and understandings of His mercy, which comes from using these two keys—*I will praise* and *whole heart*. What an exciting journey we have ahead as we pick up these keys.

Let's pray through this psalm. Even if you are feeling, "I just don't feel like praising," well, this is why we will pick up these keys and use them. Make this prayer below your exercise. We can pray this prayer completely from Psalm 9 and say these words out loud. Do not worry about feeling something on the inside or not feeling moved. I promise the more we open our mouth and pray this prayer out loud, our emotions, soul, and inner man will begin to feel a bubbling up of thankfulness and praise. Why? Because these words are alive, and they will begin to work and shift the very core of deep feelings and emotions until they line up with this prayer straight from Psalm 9. Don't rush this process. Stay on this psalm for a while.

Then, open your psalm journal and write down three wonderful things that you can remember God doing in your life. Start with three, but leave room for ten because the more you write down, the more you will remember. And between every wonderful deed that you write down, pray the first part of this psalm out loud. "I will praise You, O Lord, with my whole heart."

Write down the strongholds that no longer hold you captive. Write down the fears you no longer have. Write down the difficulties that, by God's grace and His strength, you have conquered. Then pick up those keys and say again out loud, "I will praise You, O Lord, with my whole heart."

For just as David begins to praise the Lord, he remembers more of the victories of God in his life. Psalm 9 becomes his testimony over the decades: "I still remember the triumphs of God in my life though they were years ago." A triumph is a victory, and the more we remember these and set our whole heart to praise the Lord, the more thankful to the Lord we actually become. This is also how we stay thankful with a desire to look for God and continue to praise Him for decades.

Don't hurry too quickly through this prayer. It is actually good to repeat some of these phrases over and over to the Lord. If you feel a lack of thankfulness and desire, then I promise this psalm and these keys are for you. Just keep praying. Don't quit. Just keep praying until you feel a breakthrough begin to encourage your heart—because this was my testimony. I know these keys work.

DAILY PRAYER

O Lord, I will praise You. I will worship You with all my heart, telling everyone, everywhere of Your wonders. I will praise You, O Lord, with my whole heart; I will tell of all Your marvelous works. I will be glad and rejoice, and I will take joy in You. You are the Most High. You are the highest. You are the most. You are the champion. You are the victor in my life today.

I will praise You, O Lord, with all of my heart, for You are active in my life today. You are the mighty God and You reign forever. I will set my heart to praise You. You come with Your wraparound presence, and darkness must flee.

I will remember the victories that You, O Lord, fought and won for me. You are my refuge. You are my stronghold. You are my hiding place, and all who are broken and all who are weary and everyone who knows Your mercy and everyone who puts their trust in You—You will not forsake them. You won't turn Your back on them. You will listen. Lord, You will hear their cry and my cry. Help me, Lord, to keep putting my trust, my hope in You.

Day 9: Write out Psalm 9

- Pray these verses out loud.
- Listen to the soaking for Psalm 9.
- Use these verses to talk to God.
- Can you remember the keys from this psalm?

I will praise You, O Lord. I will tell the world about Your unforgettable deeds.

Notes

1. David Guzik, "Psalm 9: God Remembers, Man Forgets," The Enduring Word Bible Commentary, https://enduringword.com/bible-commentary/psalm-9.

Day 10

You Will Not Forget

*Lord, you seem so far away when evil is near! Why do you stand
so far off as though you don't care? Why have you hidden
yourself when I need you the most?*
—Psalm 10:1 TPT

*Lord, you know and understand all the hopes of the humble and will
hear their cries and comfort their hearts, helping them all!*
—Psalm 10:17 TPT

Have you ever needed God to break into a situation when you cried out for His help and yet you still felt distant and alone? We just prayed through Psalm 9: "God, You care about us. You are personal to our lives today. You are the God who rescues us." And then we turn the page and suddenly we have this groan, this cry coming from David: "Where are You? Why are You hiding?" Psalm 10 is the very opposite. Psalm 10 is like a 180-degree turn from the previous psalm. It presents a very different cry from David, because most of David's writings reveal that God is near and that He bends down to listen to our cries. So we find David starting off this psalm with a very different cry: "It feels like You are just a spectator in my life. It feels as if You are only watching from a distance, and I need You. I need You as a refuge and I need You to rescue."

This is the very reason I love the Psalms. Because no matter where each of us are on the emotional scale of pain, we can open the Psalms and find words already written down, tried and true, and these words give us language for our deepest cries when words fail us. When we have no words to pray because of walking through loss, those times when our loved ones are sick, those hopeless seasons when life throws us a curveball we were not expecting. David is so raw with his emotions and so truthful with his feelings that this is the reason why one of the most read books of the Bible is the Psalms.

We tend to feel that if we ask these questions that David was asking, we are somehow weak, and that it is not good to be honest and ask. I feel that Solomon got it right when he wrote Ecclesiastes 3:

> *To everything there is a season, a time for every purpose under heaven...a time to weep, and a time to laugh; a time to mourn, and a time to dance...a time to gain, and a time to lose; a time to keep, and a time to cast away* (Ecclesiastes 3:1,4,6).

Right when it feels the darkest, when life looks the bleakest, we can open the Psalms and find the words we need. Here lies our first key in Psalm 10—*when God seems distant*. When the pain of distance arises, pick up this key and use it to pray the very words that David prayed: "Lord, You seem so far away and darkness seems so near. Why have You hidden Yourself when I need You the most?" This is not a key that most of us will have to use often; however, some will. But this key, these words from Psalm 10:1 will give us language to talk to God. We always need to be able to keep our conversation ongoing with God in the hardest and bleakest of times so bitterness and offense have no landing place. This is where we pick up our key and pray the very words that David prayed. These very words were inspired by the spirit of God, I believe, to keep the hurting soul connected to God through prayer. This key of praying David's words will help the heart and soul stay connected to the source of all healing—our God—instead of falling into the wasteland of bitterness. When we have no words of our own, pick up this key from Psalm 10:1 and pray these words.

What is so beautiful about this heart wrenching plea is that it seems to begin to tug on David's heart. For he begins to see those in a worse plight than his own. It is as if the very real pain and distance he was crying out of may have been the very thing that caused him to cry out for the broken and needy, for the poor and the helpless—for surely, they felt the distance too. Surely they felt just like David. Who would be their voice?

This is our next key—*the cry for justice*. The honest and raw emotions in David's prayer have now in one breath turned to justice for the oppressed. He begins to take up their cause. He begins to call out the wicked man, reminding God of those who, in their pride, do not care about God. Those who believe that God does not see their evil, God does not care about their wicked ways, or God is not real anyway, so there is nothing God can or will do to stop their evil ways.

David is now in full-on intercession for the justice of God to break in and rescue the poor and the orphan, the broken and the oppressed. He cries out, "Arise, O Lord, get up and make things right." This word *arise* can mean "stand up, get up, come on the scene and don't forget the helpless" (Strong's H6965). David is praying, "God, arise, get up, and make things right."

The passionate plea that David started off within this psalm has now made its way to a cry of intercession for the broken and the helpless. Again, I am in awe of the way the Spirit of the Lord moves on the heart of David, how He moves on the heart of every believer who will keep an ongoing lifeline of prayer to God in the hardest of times. For in the same way God began to move on David's heart for the broken and for those who seem to have no voice, He will move on our hearts. Just as suddenly as David's pain was given over to passionate pleas for the broken and forgotten with the burden of intercession heavy on his heart, it is as if confidence arises and he prays for God to arise.

Oh, the beauty of Psalm 10. Oh, the need for these Psalms to help us pray in our own personal struggles and times of grief. This psalm becomes a road map of personal healing and confidence; it simply begins with that first key—our honest, raw cry of emotion using the very words of David: "Where are You, God?" There have been times in my own personal life, as I was walking through life's twists and turns, when things happened that I did not expect and I became hurt. I did not want to pray. But without prayer, my pain made me angry, then my anger made me bitter; my bitterness started a cycle in which I began to treat people worse than I had been treated myself. It took some time to walk that backward and find the healing that only comes from a relationship and trust in the Lord. It was years ago, and I did not know about this first key—*when God seems distant.* However, today I do, and I use it. For by simply praying what David prayed—"God, You seem so far away. Why do You hide Yourself when I need You most?"—to pray those living words out loud will lead us straight to picking up the second key—*justice*.

Then David does what he always does best—he prays himself right back to the truth. He prays himself right out of any distance that he started with at the beginning of Psalm 10. Now his confession is that God will hear the cries of the poor, the orphan, the oppressed, and the broken, and He will comfort their hearts. God will hear David's cry and God will hear our cry. Simply praying David's prayer in the first verse will lead us straight to the key to pray for justice for those around us. The outcome of using these keys is our confidence level in God grows deeper and stronger. There is a realization that we truly were never far from God. He was and is always surrounding us. Spurgeon says it so beautifully, "The refiner is never far from the mouth of the furnace when his gold is in the fire, and the Son of God is always walking in the midst of the flames when his holy children are cast into them."[1]

This psalm begins with a cry, a groan of despair, but ends with David having great confidence in the judgments and the justice of God. This psalm invites us to embrace and own our pain yet keep a constant ongoing conversation with God. This will help us make a turn—instead of an inward focus of "poor me," this key will turn us to prayer, and we will be able to see those in a worse plight than ourselves. This is the promise of Psalm 10. When we also have great confidence in the judgments and justice of God, it will stir us to be a voice.

I want to encourage you to take some time as you pray through this prayer. Take time to say the phrases again and again. These are things our mind does not grasp when we only say them once, especially in seasons of pain. Say these words out loud; they are taken straight from Psalm 10. Dive in at the very beginning of your pain; please do not wait until you feel strong—that never works. We can pick up these keys that David used and walk our hearts right into healing and confidence, and we pray out loud these living words so that we end strong even before the conflict is over or before any resolution. It is simply because we are praying the inspired Word of God that David was able to grasp and write down for us.

This is also a great time to write in your journal thoughts you have at the beginning of this prayer. I encourage you to write this psalm out and pray it loud. Find a translation that you love, or even mix different translations together. That is what I did on this prayer below. Then write down the victory points as God begins to move upon your heart with justice.

DAILY PRAYER

Lord, You seem so far away when darkness is so near. It seems like You stand so far away. It's like You hide Yourself just when I need You most. God, I feel like You are hiding, and this is when I need You. Lord, I feel like You are only watching me from a distance. I feel alone, and I need You.

Oh God, the wicked boast saying, "God doesn't care what we do. There's nothing to worry about." They say, "He doesn't see it. He doesn't know it." But You do see it God. So arise, reveal Your justice and show Your power. I know You won't forget the orphans. You will not forget the helpless. You will arise on their behalf.

Oh God, remember the humble. Remember those bowed down low. You know and understand all the hopes of the humble man. You will hear their cry, Lord, You will comfort their hearts. You will help them all, and no one is left out. No one is forgotten. You do care God.

Break the power of the wicked men—all their plots and evil plans—search them out, God, shut them down.

I am crying out to You, God. You are the One who hears my cry. You hear my cry for justice and. You could never forget the helpless. You could never forget the oppressed. They're in Your heart. You will never forget the orphan. You will never forget the poor. God, You will not forget. You are my God who never forgets.

Day 10: Write out Psalm 10

- Pray these verses out loud.

- Listen to the soaking for Psalm 10.

- Use these verses to talk to God.

- Can you remember the keys from this psalm?

I know You won't forget the orphan.
You will not forget the helpless.
You will arise on their behalf.

NOTES

1. Charles Spurgeon, *The Treasury of David*, "Psalm 10, verse 1," https://archive.spurgeon.org/treasury/treasury.php.

Day 11

Song of the Steadfast

In the Lord I seek refuge.
—Psalm 11:1

Yet the Eternal One is never shaken. ...He is closely watching everything that happens. ...But remember this: the Righteous Lord loves what is right and just, and every godly one will come into his presence and gaze upon his face!
—Psalm 11:4,7 TPT

Here we are on one of my favorite psalms—Psalm 11. We have walked through ten psalms together. Each psalm provides us with life-giving keys that will equip and strengthen us deep on the inside in our daily lives. To pick up these keys and use them means we are picking up these Scriptures and praying them out loud. We are using these same prayers that David prayed from his own meditations. They are tried and true. They are tested and sure to work in us the same inner strength that they worked within David. These prayers will bring clarity and peace through every crisis and every battle. These are the prayers that David prayed and God heard. God strengthened and delivered. So expect the very same thing. The Word of God is mighty and powerful. It speaks to us as we pray and sing it out loud. This is what happened to David in Psalm 11. He was led by an inner peace that caused him to stand in crisis and know God was his protection.

As we dive into Psalm 11, we see a young David in Saul's court circled by his friends, and they are telling him to run because of imminent danger. *Kidner Classic Commentaries* writes, "This is a psalm that comes straight from a crisis."[1] In Psalm 11, David follows his heart instead of the advice of his friends.

Spurgeon gives this psalm the title "The Song of the Steadfast."[2] I can almost hear David singing these words to steady his thoughts: "It's the song of the steadfast one with the steadfast heart. I am the one with the steadfast heart and this is my song." *Steadfast* means loyal, faithful, devoted, or dedicated. It's the song of the loyal one with the faithful heart. I am the one with the devoted heart, the dedicated heart, and this dedication becomes my devotion as I sing to God. It is like he wrote out his testimony and set it to music as he is singing over himself.

Psalm 11 was most likely written at the end of First Samuel 18 when David, along with his friends, began to feel the resentment that Saul had toward him. In this chapter we find David with his friends as they compare him to a defenseless, hunted bird. They begin to tell him, "David, there is a bow and arrow pointed straight at you. You have now become like a hunted bird. So, flee—be like a bird and fly high away high in the mountains and hide yourself. You need a hiding place." Now, we know that for years David ran from Saul, living captive or as a hunted man in the land where he was born. But for whatever reason at *this time*, David said to his friends, "No, I will not run. The Lord is my refuge. He alone is my only hiding place."

Wow, what a statement! And here lies our first key for Psalm 11—*the Lord is my refuge*. The very first statement that David makes at the beginning of this psalm is written in bold letters on the front of this key. Wherever you go, take this key. Keep it close to you. Do not lose this key. It is a very important key for living, and it works every time you need it. Look at this key every single day and always say this out loud—*the Lord is my refuge*.

If we can grasp anything out of Psalm 11, let it be that this key empowers our inner man to not flee in fear but stand in faith. *The Lord is my refuge*. He really is our only refuge. *The Passion Translation* says: "I have made you my only hiding place." The New Living Translation says, "I trust in the Lord for protection."

This one statement was life changing to me. Especially, in 2020, as the whole world is in fear of this global pandemic called COVID-19. This is in every place, every nation, every state, and every city; it has changed life as we know it and shut the world down. On top of COVID-19, we have injustice in our communities, riots in our cities, California has fires burning uncontrollably, and one can feel fear everywhere. In Psalm 11, we see a young David—remember, he would have been fairly young in this season of his life. This young David had an *unmovable* faith in God. He does not give in to the warning of his friends. He is basically saying, "If God is in the middle of trouble, then I will stay in the middle because God is here. If God is in the middle of the shakings of life, then I too will stay right in the middle. If God is here, I am staying because this is where my refuge is. Why would I ever run? Why would I flee to the mountains if my refuge is in the middle of the crisis?"

Now, I cannot remember a time in my life when everyone around me was encouraging me in one thing because of great danger and I said, "No, I will stay here." But I can remember times in my life when I was like David's friends, encouraging someone with great passion to run. "Get out of town, trouble is coming. Run for your life." So this psalm reminds me again to take a step back, pray, ask the Lord for His counsel, and *then* give my counsel to friends.

David says, "In the Lord I put my trust. I flee to Him for protection. He is who I confide in. He is who I have hope in, and I will flee to Him for refuge."

When faith arises, it bubbles up from within. We begin to feel bold and courageous. But when fear arises, it presses down like a heavy weight. This fear will cause people to run before they think things through, and it will continue to encourage the fearful soul to *keep* running. Once we listen to the voice of fear, it has an open door to our soul, and we will just keep running because it always says, "*Run!*" Have you ever met someone, and they fear everything and everyone? I believe that fear can be broken, but we have to pick up this key and pray what David prayed—in the Lord I take refuge. Fear will feed on our emotions, which empowers our soul to fear even more. When we look up the word *soul*, we see that emotions, desires, appetites are all part of the soul. That is why we want to pick up this key—*in the Lord I take refuge.*

We want to say these words out loud as many times as necessary. We want to say, out loud, these words that are alive and full of living power. These words will build you up and convince you of their truth. These words spoken out loud will build up faith, empower the heart, enlarge our faith, and then *we* tell our soul to get in line with the Word of God. David spoke to his soul. He told it what to do: "Bless the Lord, O my soul" (Ps. 103:1); "Awake, O my soul" (Ps. 57:8 TPT).

We need to pick up our faith-building key found in Psalm 11 called *the Lord is my refuge*. When that instinct to run hits our soul, or fear comes in so overwhelming, we can take a step back; take a long, deep breath because maybe He is saying something different. "*Stay, I am right here.*" The Lord is my refuge. David was able to hear this when his friends were not. His friends were looking at the situation; David was looking at his refuge.

The power of the Word of God combined with it being said on his lips. Maybe that is why David could see something greater than the situation at hand. He was able to see his place of safety was right in the middle of Saul's court. David saw God there. He looked higher and saw that God was reigning. He is on His throne. His eyes are on the righteous. He is the eternal One who never sleeps and never slumbers. He is reigning, and He is also watching.

And here lies our second key for Psalm 11. We find this amazing, powerful key in verse 4. I am calling this key, *God is never shaken*. The New Living Translation says, "The Lord still rules from heaven," and the New King James Version says, "The Lord's throne is in heaven." He reigns from His throne. He rules from His throne, and He is never shaken sitting on His throne. What an unbelievable promise. No matter what we face, even the times we want to look up to the heavens and say, "God, do You see this? Do You see what is happening?" This is our key. We can pray with confidence because this is the truth—*God is never shaken*. He is on His governmental throne and He is reigning. He is making decrees about our life from this throne.

And He is closely watching everything that happens. Spurgeon writes, "What plots can men devise which Jesus will not discover?"[3] It is all in His gaze, for with a glance His eyes examine every heart. Nothing that happens in our lives goes unnoticed by the Lord.

So what are the circumstances in your life? For if there has been hardship, conflict, battles, judgments, you can pick up these keys and bring them into your battle so that there is a response of faith instead of a reaction of fear. This first key, *the Lord is my refuge,* will cause you to look up. And as you look up you will see the second key at work for *God is never shaken.* He is never taken by surprise. God never says, "On no, I did not expect that!" He rules from His throne.

So grab hold of these powerful keys, because when used we have a beautiful promise. There is a response from Heaven when these two keys are jingling in the hands of believers and applied to the door of every heart. Our promise is the very last verse of this psalm. "Every godly one will come into his presence and gaze upon his face."[4] What a promise! We *will behold*—that can mean we will see, we will perceive; it means to see as a seer in the ecstatic state. It means we see by experience. We see His face. We experience His presence. In the beatitudes, Jesus says the pure in heart will see His.

Oh, let me encourage you to set aside time to meditate on Psalm 11. Sing this psalm, pray this psalm, decree this psalm, and I believe that He will fling wide the door to His presence, the door of encounter. For David writes, "every godly one will come into His presence and gaze upon His face." This is your promise. It was true of David and it is true for us. In this place of beholding His face, He will show you the next step. There is a greater awareness of His presence, so we will hear His voice more clearly. We will have greater perception; we will have greater insight. It is "in the middle"—sometimes our greatest insights, our greatest encounters are right in the middle of the crisis. Start expecting to behold the beauty, the power, the strength, the glory, and the worth of God, and what we behold in Him begins to *shine* through us.

DAILY PRAYER

Lord, in the season of crisis and all through the conflict, I ask that You, oh God, reveal Yourself to me as a refuge, as my hiding place, as the Eternal One on the throne with Your eyes watching my whole situation. As You gaze at my heart would You give me great wisdom in how to walk forward?

Lord, when I find myself in times of testing like David in Psalm 11—if good friends or even peers would ever say to me, "Run, leave, and find a hiding place"—let my answer be the same as David's. I have made the Lord my only hiding place. You are my only safe place and my only refuge. This is why I sing, and this song leads me to trust. I will sing this chorus over my own life, just like David did. It's the song of the steadfast one with the steadfast heart. Lord, I'm the one with the steadfast heart, and this is my song.

Lord, You are never shaken seated on Your heavenly throne, reigning as Lord and King over all, so I lift my eyes to the Lord, and here is faith and confidence in times of testing—it's here I see Your face, oh God. Thank You that when there is great testing and I feel my faith being stretched, that I take refuge in You.

Thank You for strength for the journey and a steady heart to keep reaching.

Day 11: Write out Psalm 11

- Pray these verses out loud.
- Listen to the soaking for Psalm 11.
- Use these verses to talk to God.
- Can you remember the keys from this psalm?

> *I lift my eyes to the Lord, and here is faith and confidence in times of testing— it's here I see Your face.*

NOTES

1. Derek Kidner, *Psalms 1-72, Kidner Classic Commentaries* (Downers Grove, IL: InterVarsity Press, 1973), 89.

2. Charles Spurgeon, *The Treasury of David*, "Psalm 11, Subject," https://archive.spurgeon.org/treasury/treasury.php.

3. Ibid., "Psalm 11, verse 4."

4. *The Passion Translation.*

Day 12

The Best of Words, the Worst of Words

*Help, O Lord, for the godly are no more; the faithful
have vanished from among men.*
—Psalm 12:1 BSB

*Everyone lies, everyone flatters, and everyone deceives. Nothing but
empty talk, smooth talk, and double-talk. Where are the truthful?*
—Psalm 12:2 TPT

*The words of the Lord are pure words; they are silver tried
in an earthen furnace refined seven times.*
—Psalm 12:6

If you have ever read *A Tale of Two Cities*, a very famous novel by
Charles Dickens, the title and first sentence of that novel could
very well be the opening sentence of Psalm 12, with a slight play
on words. "It was the best of words; it was the worst of words—a
tale of two kings." Most commentaries place David serving in Saul's
court at the writing of this psalm. It could have very well been in the
same season that he wrote Psalm 11. We have David surrounded by
those serving in Saul's court; however, David calls them *his* enemies.

He makes it crystal clear that those around him were liars, with flattering tongues that said one thing in the presence of David and the total opposite when they were talking to each other or to the king himself. They wanted the king's favor for themselves and would do or say anything to get it.

David starts this psalm with a very real plea and cry: "Help, Lord." Other translations say, "Save me, O God." He writes, "I have looked everywhere and there is no one anywhere who is faithful. There is not one at all who is righteous, not one who is truthful; they have all *vanished* from the earth. They are all gone. I have looked everywhere and there is not one faithful person alive on the earth." He writes, "There is no one around me who speaks anything truthful. Everyone speaks with their empty talk, their smooth talk, and double-talk." He asks the question, "Where are the truthful?" Spurgeon writes about this season of David's life: "The Psalmist sees the extreme danger of his position, for a man had better be among lions than among liars."[1]

So David is in a very different kind of a battle. This was not a battle that he could win fighting with his sword and wraparound shield. This was a battle of words; for while he was in Saul's court there were circumstances that were happening behind the scenes. David was up against very real jealously, anger, and discontentment among Saul's servants in the palace. There were rumors, lies, vicious untruths being said and spread about him, and there was no one who stood up for David. There was no one to speak up for his honor and his reputation. There was no one who would stand up for truth.

What David did next is what I love most about him. He wholeheartedly turned to the Lord. He begins to write this beautiful contrasting picture between the *worst of words*—which were lies, rumors, and jealousy from those who were against David—compared to the complete opposite, *the best of words*—the truth, the gold, the purity the Word of God, which was from God Himself.

If you have ever been the target of slander, lies, or rumors, it is a bit like COVID-19, the mother of all viruses in the year 2020. Once this virus gets out, it keeps spreading and causing harm and even death. There is no stopping a virus. It keeps growing and moving as it expectantly looks for a new host, and we never really know that this very aggressive virus is looking to jump on our back creating havoc of all kinds. To answer this type of virus in your own self-defense will never work because people believe what they want to believe. We have one option, just like David had one option. We have to turn to the Lord like David did. If we are going to talk about our words, then we also need to talk about our tweets, our threads, our texts, and our postings to social media.

A long time ago, I made the terrible mistake of Googling my name. Well, that never ends well. (#neverdothat!) I was in shock at the ridiculous lies, rumors, the name calling, the quotes that I never said. The things people wrote about me, and about many amazing people I know, were horrible. I thought, "Who in their right mind has this much time on their hands to actually post and write on social media complete lies that were never ever said?" In that moment, I found myself in the battle of Psalm 12. I call these word battles the civil war on our character and our life before God. Our only help is going to come from one place, and this is where we use our first key—*Help, Lord. Save me.*

David cries out, "Save me, Lord." The context of this word *save* throughout the *Tanakh* (Old Testament) is "to rescue someone from his enemy, a trouble or illness." This is the same word used in Deuteronomy 20:4. Maybe David was thinking or maybe he was singing this very Scripture from his meditations. He could have been saying, "God, in the same way that Moses called out for You to save him—God, save me in the same way!" Can you hear David singing the below Scripture?

> For the Lord your God is he that goeth with you, to fight for you against your enemies, to **save** you (Deuteronomy 20:4 KJV).

We can add that the Greek for "save" can mean "preservation, salvation" related to *sōs* "safe, healthy." David is sending out an SOS to God asking for help, asking to be rescued, and for God to preserve his life and keep him safe and healthy.[2]

Spurgeon writes, "He therefore turns himself to his all-sufficient Helper, the Lord, whose help is never denied to his servants, and whose aid is enough for all their needs."[3] God never denies David. And God will never deny us. God never said to anyone, "I will not help you."

So if we find ourselves among men falling away from God and see ourselves in a web of controversy, let us pick up the key that David used—*Help, Lord. Save me.* Say these words out loud. Pray them—*Help, Lord. Save me.* There is only one way to put every false truth to rest, and it is appealing to the Lord, asking Him to step into your life in such a way that all the swirling "worst words" are once and for all silenced. God can do this. God will do this. Send out your SOS to God that He will save you and keep you safe.

This psalm started with the *worst of words*, but it will end with the *best of words*. For the appeal that David made to God in the first verses, we find the answer and the exact opposite near the end. Here we find the best of words. These are the purest of words. Here lies our second key for Psalm 12—*pure and purified words*.

In verse 6, we see that these words are anything but empty. They are the complete opposite of the deceptive and proud lies being spoken by the faithless. These words are the perfect word of God, the Torah.

> "The words of the Lord are pure words;" that is, pure, chaste, and, as the Hebrew implies, not dyed, or counterfeit, but sincere and trustworthy, as "Silver tried by the fire;" that is, like the purest silver in sound, weight, and color...not only in the fire, "But purged from the earth;" that is, approved of by the most versed in the trade of gold and silver.[4]

The word *refine* means "to bring to a fine or a pure state free from impurities through smelting or testing." These words are tested and prove true. They are refined, purged by the fire so that the silver is separated from the dross. The dross is the less than desirable part; it is impure and thrown away. These words are examined, and this is not just one time, but this process is done seven times, meaning it was purged and refined over and over and over and proven true.

The *worst of words* are complete dross. They are filled with no substance; they are not proven nor tried by the fire, spoken by the faithless who only live for personal gain and popularity. These words are impure and thrown away. They are not examined, and they are spoken from those who believe that their lips are their own and they will say what they want, declaring, "Who can stop us?"

David fought this war of words by turning to his all-sufficient helper, the Lord. He used the best of words to lean into and trust. His battle plan was to pick up his keys, turn to the Lord with an appeal and groan of *Help, Lord. Save me.* Then he trusted in the *pure and purified words.*

If this is you, move in the direction that David moved. Don't be fooled by the worst of words. As we pray this psalm, we will find our peace, no matter what has been said or no matter what has happened. I want to invite you to pick up these keys that David used and begin to cry out to the Lord and lean into the tried and true Word of God. There is something about rumors and gossip that strikes and wounds the human heart and soul. But we have an antidote, we have a prescription, and it is the Word of God. It is Psalm 12 for all manner of gossip. It is the truth found in the Word. So let us do what David did and turn away from the lying lips. Lift up a cry to the Lord as you turn toward the Word that is purified and gold. This Word of God is alive, and it will strengthen us. It strengthens us from the inside out as we pray these words out.

DAILY PRAYER

Lord, remind me of the power of the written Word of God. I ask that You would help me forgive anyone who has spoken against me. Lord, forgive me if I have been the one speaking the worst of words about anyone else. For my lips are not my own. You see and hear everything.

God, help me to do what David did. Help me to pick up these keys. Help me, Lord, for the godly are no more and we are watching the faithful fall and vanish right before our eyes. Help me when everyone flatters with their words, empty talk, empty words God, where are the faithful? Where are the truthful?

So I turn to You, God; You are my all-sufficient helper. You never deny me. Lord, Your help is what I need. You will always help me when You hear my cry. I move Your way. You are the mighty One who saves me. You always listen for me. Your help is what I need. Your words are true. Your words are pure. Your words are right, God. They are clean and sure.

Day 12: Write out Psalm 12

- Pray these verses out loud.
- Listen to the soaking for Psalm 12.
- Use these verses to pray when the worst of words arise.
- What are the keys from this psalm?

> *I turn to You, God; You are my all-sufficient helper. You never deny me. Your help is what I need.*

NOTES

1. Charles Spurgeon, *The Treasury of David*, "Psalm 12, verse 1," https://archive.spurgeon.org/treasury/treasury.php.

2. From *soizein*; Joseph Meyer, formerly a Doctoral Fellow in Classical Languages and Literature at UCSB.

3. Spurgeon, *The Treasury of David*, "Psalm 12, verse 1."

4. Saint Robert Bellarmine, John O'Sullivan, trans., *A Commentary on the Book of Psalms* (St. Athanasius Press, 2018), 60.

Day 13

The "How Long" Psalm

*How long, O Lord? Will You forget me forever? How long will
You hide Your face from me? How long shall I take counsel in my soul,
having sorrow in my heart daily? How long will my enemy be exalted
over me? Consider and hear me, O Lord my God; enlighten my eyes...
I have trusted in Your mercy...I will sing to the Lord, because
He has dealt bountifully with me.*
—Psalm 13:1-3,5-6 NKJV

Have you ever prayed to the Lord, "How long? How long, O
Lord?" Have you prayed the words in Psalm 13 with such
anguish that you could feel this groan in your belly, just
like David?

This is not about "how long" until dinner is ready. Or "how long"
until we get there? Or "how long" until the movie starts? Or "how
long" until this project is done? This is not that. This is a gut-wrench-
ing cry that comes up from a deep place on the inside, and in agony
there is a groan toward Heaven with a cry of "How long?" This groan
is felt deeply because there is a very real knowledge of distance and
separation. David felt as if God had left him alone and totally forgotten him, and in reality it was the opposite. David felt that God had

forgotten him. He felt that God was choosing to distance Himself from David. David also writes about this separation of "How long" in Psalm 22. Jesus actually quotes word for word from Psalm 22 as He also felt the separation, the distance from God, when He was on the cross.

As I began to sing and study Psalm 13, I began to ponder the patriarchs of old and asked myself the question: "Who among them would have cried out to God in this same manner? *How long?*" Could David possibly have remembered this two-word cry from his meditations on Scripture? Was there a prayer that made an imprint on his heart so that he also cried out to God with these same two words, *how long?*

When we look back to the Torah, the very first passionate cry of "How long?" was *not* from man to God, but it was the opposite. It was from God to man. We see this in Exodus 10:3 when Moses and Aaron went to Pharaoh and said to him, "Thus saith the Lord God of the Hebrews, *How long* wilt thou refuse to humble thyself before me? let my people go, that they may serve me" (KJV).

The Cambridge Commentary writes, "The phrase 'how long' is not a request for data concerning a time-table; rather it is a statement of *impatient hope.* Not only is the present circumstance unbearable; it cannot be endured, and it need not last if YHWH will simply pay attention."[1]

In Exodus 16:28, the Lord said to Moses, "*How long* refuse ye to keep my commandments and my laws?" (KJV). We find this same question from God to man in Numbers and also in Joshua. We find this cry at least four different times in Job as Job asks this question, "How long?" Now, David would have known this cry. He would have had this cry and petition memorized with his knowledge of the Torah. This is a question that man asks God but also the question that God continually asks man: "How long?" In fact, these two words, *how long*, were the very two words that God asked Samuel when he was grieving Saul's disobedience. God uses these same two words in First Samuel 16:1: "*How long* will you mourn for Saul, since I have rejected him from ruling over Israel? Fill your horn with oil and go. I will send you to Jesse the Bethlehemite, for I have chosen a king for Myself from among his sons." God had found a man after His own heart, and this young man proved to have a heart for God. We benefit from his writings and his heart because we can simply pray his prayers and know that God is listening and He will answer.

Kidner Classic Commentaries calls this psalm *Desolation into Delight*. He also states. "No doubt the divine 'forgetting' and 'hiding the face' meant *the withholding of practical help* (since in the Old Testament God's 'remembering' and 'seeing' are not states of consciousness but preludes to action), but the real hurt of it was personal, if we may judge from David's constant longing to 'behold (God's) face.'"[2] David understood that this distance he felt from God would prove true, that there would be a withholding of practical help. David needed all the help he could get—therefore, his plea of "How long?"

In Psalm 13, we find David using this cry no less than four different times in a row. It is a very revealing psalm about David's intense desire for fellowship with God and his despair when he could not feel the presence of God.

So here lies our first key—*how long*?" For this reason, I love the Psalms. Each chapter provides language for us to use to talk to God in every difficult season. It is OK to ask God the hard questions:

"How long?" Use this key in hard seasons when you want answers but they don't seem to be coming. Use this key, *"How long?"* in the same way that Psalm 10 helps us walk through difficult times of feeling a distance from God. These verses help us ask God the hard questions when we do not have our own words or when life is hard.

But the mistake many people make in these hard and intense seasons is they stop right in the middle of the first couple of verses and land right here. It is imperative that we pick up this key, *how long*, and in honesty use these verses to talk to God—but *keep walking*. Keep Psalm 13 close to your heart so that you do not stay in the very first couple of verses. Don't get off on an exit ramp for greener pastures, because there are not *any* in these first two verses. Just stay steady and keep walking.

In Psalm 13:2, David writes, "How long must I take counsel in my soul?" (ESV). Now, this is *not* a key; this is a "heads up." For our soul is our core of emotions; it is the seat of our appetites, our desires, our mind (Strong's H5315). Most of the time if not *all* of the time, our soul is 100 percent wrong about our situations. So if we are taking counsel from our soul, this can actually lead us in the very opposite direction of truth and reality. To take counsel is to listen and be led by our soul, which will not keep us steady and reach for truth. It actually means to be led by our desires and the seat of our appetites. That sounds so scary to me. My soul is what I wholeheartedly do *not* want to follow. We need to pray the Word of God and we tell our soul to get in line; we do not ever ask our soul what it thinks. Our soul will always be a bit of a "Debbie Downer." So we use the words of Scripture in our mouth and speak the Word of God out loud. We tell our soul to line up with the Word of God. We never ask our soul to counsel us.

After these four *how longs,* David prays a very important prayer in verse 3 that will lead him straight into the heart of God, and here lies our second key—*enlighten my eyes.* Right here lies a very important prayer that becomes the turning point in this psalm. And this is really what David does best. I wonder if, in all of his meditations in the Torah (the first five books of the Bible), did he learn about this necessary turn, or pivot, where he starts off in despair and honesty before God, then makes this turn *to* God. Did he see this in his meditations and know that God had an answer and that God would answer? I don't know, but David helps us pray in these difficult seasons. David's prayer to God, when he prays, "Enlighten my eyes" or "Give light to my eyes" means "Give me a greater knowledge and understanding about what's happening." It means, "Inform me or tell me and make me aware of what You're doing and where You are." May we pray the exact same prayer that David prayed when our season begins with *how long.*

This is a very important prayer because we need the light of God to shine upon us when we feel a real distance from God. We actually see in Ephesians 1:17-19 that Paul prays this very prayer. Paul prays that the God of our Lord Jesus Christ, the Father of glory, would give to you and me the spirit of wisdom and revelation in the knowledge of Jesus. That the eyes of our understanding would be enlightened. Paul is praying, "God, open up our eyes. God, teach me, instruct me. Let our eyes be opened so that we have an understanding of the knowledge of Jesus, of who He is, but also a living understanding of what God is doing and what we are walking through today so that our hearts respond to God in a right way. So that our hearts are not closed to God in feeling a distance but that we have a revelation of what God is doing in these seasons and therefore our hearts remain open and looking for this living understanding."

Psalm 13 is a song that will give us language. It will give us words to keep our heart connected with the fact that God has not gone anywhere though we feel a very real separation. These keys—*how long* and *enlighten our eyes*—will keep us in an ongoing communication with God, much like we walked through in Psalm 10, so that our prayers and our conversation with God never ever cease, even when we do not comprehend fully what is happening.

However, even though the feeling of distance is real, the truth is—God is always with you. He will never leave you, though it feels like there is a distance. He is close. This is our eternal promise. "But Zion said, The Lord hath forsaken me, and my Lord hath forgotten me. Can a woman forget her sucking child, that she should not have compassion on the son of her womb? yea, they may forget, yet will I not forget thee. Behold, I have graven thee upon the palms of my hands."[3] We see in Psalm 139 that God cares about us so much He has everything about us written down in His book. We also see in Psalm 56 that God so cares about us that He catches every one of our tears in His bottle. This is our promise. He cares. He is attentive to our cries even in the distance.

Those first two keys—*how long* and *enlighten our eyes*—will keep us on a steady path through verse 4 and then straight into verses 5 and 6. These two keys will empower our prayer life to keep walking and not quit all through the questions. There is a day of breakthrough that meets us at the end of this psalm. As we walk through the struggle and the wrestle between truth and false words, the false begins to subside and truth always wins. Therefore, the last two verses can be prayed out strong and loud as our inner man is strengthened.

So picture David, and then maybe picture yourself on this same journey. David picks up these keys—*how long* and *enlighten our eyes*—and he asks God the hard questions. He has a request: "God, enlighten my eyes, help me to understand." He stays focused and keeps walking right into this testimony: "I have trusted in Your mercy...I will sing to the Lord, because He has dealt bountifully with me." I love these two verses in *The Passion Translation*:

> *Lord, I have always trusted in your kindness, so answer me. I will yet celebrate with passion and joy when your salvation lifts me up. I will sing my song of joy to you, the Most High, for in all of this you have strengthened my soul. My enemies say that I have no Savior, but I know that I have one in you!*

The last two verses of Psalm 13 are totally opposite from the two verses of the beginning of this psalm. There is a shift, and David begins to sing and declare, "I have trusted in Your mercy." It is as if this song that he was singing began to literally wash over his heart and his soul and he came to a place of complete confidence and trust in the Word. For as he sang, "I have always trusted in your kindness. I will celebrate with passion and joy, for He has dealt bountifully with me," we can see that this actually became true in his heart. These were not mere words of a song; this became the truth that he was living. When he looked back over his dark and hard season of *how long*, the song of remembrance that he began to sing was, "I have trusted in Your mercy. God, all through the hardships and all through the delays, I will celebrate because even there You have dealt bountifully with me."

David begins to sing, "My heart shall rejoice." Right here, he is telling his emotions and his heart to listen to the word that he is declaring. David begins to sing the word over his emotions and over his heart—instead of letting his emotions and heart take control of him. He begins to say, "I'm going to rejoice because of the salvation of God. I will sing over my heart and soul and they will listen and line up with the Word of God."

Spurgeon wrote about this; he said, "There is not half enough singing in the world...I remember a servant who used to sing while she was at the wash-tub. Her mistress said to her, 'Why, Jane, how is it that you are always singing?' She said, 'It keeps the bad thoughts away.'"[4]

If this is you and your song literally keeps the bad thoughts away, then keep singing. That is what David did. Be like David—sing and tell your heart, "You will rejoice in the salvation of God, for God has dealt bountifully with me." This song leads David to the truth— "God has dealt bountifully with me." This is the truth, and this is the reality of David's season.

At the beginning of this psalm, David is in deep distress in his life; he cries out, "How long?" but now he is remembering the mercy and the loving kindness and the salvation of God. He is remembering how God has dealt with him abundantly and bountifully. In this remembrance, he begins to sing a song of thankfulness. As he is singing, his emotions are lining up with what he is singing, which is the truth of the Word of God. Also, his body has come into alignment with this truth. It's the power of singing the Scriptures, and one David Guzik writes, "We need to realize that our feelings are not giving us full and accurate information."[5] But if we will actually take this psalm, pray it, sing it, and cry out to the Lord, we will walk right into the truth that the Lord is near and He will strengthen us. It was the testimony of David, and it will be the testimony in our song. The truth is, God never forgets us. He has engraved us in the palm of His hand. We are never forgotten. You can simply read Psalm 139 and see that He knows every tiny detail about our lives.

We are not forgotten. We are chosen.

DAILY PRAYER

How long. How long. How long. How long. O God?

This is a question on my heart—these two words, "How long?" How long will it seem like You have forgotten me, God? It seems You look the other way. I am in need. All the shaking in my soul, all this daily sorrow—how long? How long, God?

Look up and answer me; take a good look at me and light up my eyes. Everywhere I turn, God, everywhere I look seems like constant darkness. It's overwhelming in my soul; there's a shaking in my soul...how long?

Feel my pleading, hear my cry. Hear my prayer, O God—how long? When everywhere I look is constant darkness—God, breathe Your life into my spirit. This is where I need Your breath of life in me.

Lord, I have always trusted in Your kindness. O Lord, Your salvation lifts me higher. I will sing my song of joy to You for through everything You strengthen me. I have found a Savior in You. When I ask "How long. How long?" I will remember—You have been good. You have been good to me.

So, Lord, in those seasons of pain and despair, in the place of needing faith and breakthrough. I ask, Lord, that as I pray this psalm, You would meet me in an unprecedented way. Let Ephesians 1:18 literally have its perfect way in my life and as I begin to sing the Word and meditate on this truth of Psalm 13; that You would shed Your perfect light into my heart. Thank You, Lord. Amen.

Day 13: Write out Psalm 13

- Pray these verses out loud.
- Listen to the soaking for Psalm 13.
- Have you ever been in a season like Psalm 13?
- Can you remember the keys from this psalm?

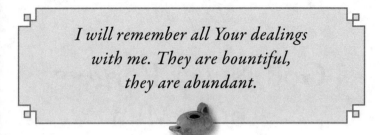

*I will remember all Your dealings
with me. They are bountiful,
they are abundant.*

Notes

1. Walter Brueggemann and William H Bellinger, Jr., *Psalms: The New Cambridge Bible Commentary* (New York: NY, Cambridge University Press, 2014), 76.

2. Kidner, *Psalms*, 93-94

3. Charles Spurgeon, *The Treasury of David*, "Psalm 13, verse 1," https://archive.spurgeon.org/treasury/treasury.php.

4. Charles Spurgeon, qtd. in David Guzik, "Psalm 13: Enlighten My Eyes," The Enduring Word Bible Commentary, https://enduringword.com/bible-commentary/psalm-13.

5. Ibid.

Day 14

God Never Forgets About Man

The fool has said in his heart, "There is no God." They are corrupt, they do abominable deeds, there is none who does good. The Lord looks down from heaven on the children of men, to see if there are any who understand, who seek God.

—Psalm 14:1-2

In 2016, I said yes to an invitation that I felt was from the Lord. It came through my amazing sons who asked me to sing my way through the Psalms. So starting in June, I began to sing through the Psalms, starting with Psalm 1, every month uploading a new psalm to our 24/7 radio. I sang straight from the Scriptures. Now the first couple of psalms were great. They were encouraging, and they were very easy to sing. Then I sat down to record Psalm 10, 11, 12, 13.... So we have these three months of singing, "God, where are You? David, run, the king wants to kill you." Then, "The faithful have fallen and are no more; I have looked and there is not one faithful on the earth." Then, "How long, God? How long will You forget me?"

So when I sat down to record Psalm 14, I remember opening my Bible to read the first verse, which was, "The fool says in his heart, 'There is no God.'" I sat back and said to myself, "Not another depressing psalm." I started flipping through the Psalms just looking for some joy. I called my son and said, "Isaac, I cannot record Psalm 14. It's so depressing, and we just need to leave it out. Let's skip this one or come back for it at a later date after a couple months of peace and joy." I remember saying, "Is it really *that* big of a deal to leave out one psalm? How do I take Psalm 14 and make it a soaking inspirational song so that people are being encouraged as they listen?" It starts with fools saying there is no God and then God is looking over the whole human race and sees no one who is even thinking about Him! I said to my son, "Who wants to soak in that?"

Well, Isaac said, "Mom, you cannot skip Psalm 14. You are singing your way through the Psalms, and you need to walk through each one, wrestle through it, find the gold, and sing about that gold."

Needless to say, this psalm was quite hard. As the *New Cambridge Bible Commentary* writes: "There is no direct address to God, no direct complaint, and no petition. It does, quite like the lament genre, champion 'the righteous,' (v. 5) and cast 'fools' as the antagonists to the righteous poor."[1] So I opened up one of my favorite commentaries on the Psalms, *The Treasury of David*. These three volumes have given my heart so much encouragement and also given my mouth a lot of language to sing. Mike Bickle, my former pastor, bought me this three-volume set in the late '90s when I said how much I love the Psalms. He said, "Read these commentaries because they are written by men and who gave their whole life in prayer, research, and study of the Psalms." So, I opened up *The Treasury of David* and turned to Psalm 14, and right in the very first paragraph, I found the gold. The gold is actually in the title itself—"For the Music Director. A Psalm of David." My thoughts did a 180 and I became so excited about Psalm 14. Spurgeon writes:

> The dedication to the Chief Musician stands at the head of fifty-three of the Psalms, and clearly indicates that such psalms were intended, not merely for the private use of believers, but to be sung in the great assemblies by the appointed choir at whose head was the overseer, or superintendent, called in our version, "the Chief Musician," and by Ainsworth, "the Master of the Music." Several of these psalms have little or no praise in them, and were not addressed directly to the Most High, and yet were to be sung in public worship; which is a clear indication that the theory of Augustine lately revived by certain hymn-book makers, that nothing but praise should be sung, is far more plausible than scriptural. Not only did the ancient Church chant hallowed doctrine and offer prayer amid her spiritual songs, but even the wailing notes of complaint were put into her mouth by the sweet singer of Israel who was inspired of God.[2]

Psalm 14 was written and intended for our local church services. Can you imagine the worship leader or song director asking everyone to stand as we sing through Psalm 14? Probably after the first line of the first verse, everyone standing would be looking around, thinking, "What are we singing this for? We have to sing praise!" Spurgeon goes on to remind us the very reason we should sing psalms like this in public worship, for Paul encouraged the Colossians to "Let the word of Christ dwell in you richly in all wisdom, teaching and admonishing one another in psalms and hymns and spiritual songs, singing with grace in your hearts to the Lord" (Col. 3:16). Let's unwrap this psalm and find the keys.

The word *fool* can mean stupid, wicked (especially impious), vile person" (Strong's H5036). It comes from another word, which has a literal meaning of "to wilt, to fall away, to fail, to sink or drop down" (Strong's H5034). So David writes in the first line stating the facts of the foolish. It is as if David wants this psalm to be sung and on the lips of all people to remind everyone, "You are a fool if you say there is no God." The vile and wicked person wants to wish God away so, in their mind, there is no consequence for sin and wickedness. In the Greek, the word for *fool* literally means "without a diaphragm." That's an idiom for being witless, stupid, or foolish—much like being "heartless" in English means to be mean and unkind.

We see here that the fool will come to no good end. He will wilt. He will fail or sink.

> David [conveys] that men in general, through the corruption
> of their intellect, had come to such a pitch of blindness, as to
> become entirely regardless of their last end, and to think there
> was no God who regarded mankind, or to whom they would
> be accountable.[3]

God says of them, "None of them do good." Spurgeon writes, "The Hebrew phrase is an utter denial concerning any mere man that he of himself doeth good. ...This is the verdict of the all-seeing Jehovah, who cannot exaggerate or mistake."[4]

Just because man refuses to believe that God is real does not make God any less real. No one can wish God away. God answers this foolishness in the second verse. His answer is an action—He looks down from Heaven. He looks down to see if anyone is truly wise or if anyone seeks God. The God whom the foolish deny is the very One looking directly into their thoughts, their life, their soul, and He is the One who determines their eternal fate. David Guzik writes, "From the italics in the New King James Version we can see that what the fool actually says is, 'No God.' 'That is, "No God for me."'"[5] There is a very real battle here between the foolish and God. But God never, ever loses. So this battle is futile. There is only one side that counts in this battle, and it is God's.

David writes in Psalm 19 that the very heavens proclaim the glory of God. The skies display His craftsmanship; the skies testify of His hands' great work. Creation itself reveals the Creator with its message going throughout the entire earth. Man can forget about God, but God never forgets about man. The very men and women who choose to forget about God, God has them engraved on the palm of His hand. Here lies our key for Psalm 14—*God never forgets about man.*

I think back on some of the patriarchs who encountered God. I think of Jacob who had his open heaven experience in Genesis 27. He saw stairs headed up to Heaven with angels ascending and descending, and he saw God at the very top. When he had this encounter, he was not in covenant with God. He was deceitful and cunning and had no fear of God. That did not matter; God chose Jacob. I think of Saul, in Acts 8 and 9, doing all he could do to destroy the Church. He watched as Stephen was martyred. He threw people in prison for their faith. He was uttering threats and eager to kill the Lord's followers. God stopped him in his tracks, and he heard the voice of God say, "Saul, Saul, why are you persecuting Me?"

I think of Nebuchadnezzar in the Book of Daniel to whom God gives dreams. In Daniel 4, he walks through the fulfillment of his dream as this chapter ends with him praising God, saying, "Now, I praise and glorify and honor the King of Heaven." He was a merciless and evil Babylonian king.

This is our key for Psalm 14. No matter what people say, *it doesn't matter*. It simply does not matter. For every foolish soul who testifies that God is not real, it does not even matter—because God is. And God could have a set time and destiny for this soul who battles against Himself, and he will lose. Let this psalm actually encourage you. Pull out this key, *God never forgets about man*, and begin to use this in prayer for every lost friend or foe. For every family member, son or daughter, sister or brother—if the words they say are from Psalm 14, use this key—*God never forgets about man*. The One who reigns supreme on the throne, the One who shines in perfection and burns with holy fire—He never forgets. There is no one so lost that the grace and mercy of God cannot chase them down.

I take Psalm 14 and pray for every lost soul I know. I name them by name. Their battle is not with us; their battle is with God. But God is real—they will never win this war. I have used this key in Psalm 14 to pray for so many people to whom God suddenly revealed the goodness of who He is and the depths of His burning passion for them. This is the beauty of Psalm 14. Pick up this key and use it often. Then watch the Kingdom of God begin to grow with those whose testimony is no longer, "God is not real."

Though man forget about God, though men say, "There is no God for me," here lies our key—*God never will forget about man.*

DAILY PRAYER

God, You are real. No man or women can wish You away. The evidence is plain; we can look around at all Creation. Oh God, though men may try to forget about You, it is You, oh God, who never will forget about man. Lord, You look down in love, bending down from the heavens. Your eyes are gazing intently upon very living being and every nation. You continue to look down with Your unending love and in Your continual mercy.

God, You are searching and looking to see if there's anyone who thinks about God. Is there anyone who wants to please God? As strong as man would wish to deny You, God, don't they realize they are battling against God? Therefore, they will never win.

So here is the truth—no man can wish God away. For the battle is not with mere men; the battle is with the Most High God, the one who knows it all. Lord, You make it very clear—though man may wish to forget about God, God never will forget about man. God never will forget about man.

And now, Lord, I take Psalm 14 and lift up every family member or friend who would say, "God is not real." Lord, break in— the same way that You broke into Jacob's life and Saul's life and the kings all throughout the Old Testament who encountered

You in dreams. Some turned and some did not. I am asking for a turning of the heart of those I lift up to You right now. May Your mercy and truth chase them down. Would You reveal Yourself to them in a dream? Would You reveal Your kindness to them? Would You help me to be a light and a testimony of the goodness of God all throughout life? God, I pick up this key, "God never forgets about man," and thank You that You never forget. Now, fling wide the door of salvation to each person on my list I am praying for and watching as You work for good in their life. Bring revelation and salvation into their hearts. In Your name, amen.

Day 14: Write out Psalm 14

- Pray these verses out loud.
- Listen to the soaking for Psalm 14.
- Use these verses to talk to God.
- Can you remember the keys from this psalm?

> *While man may wish to forget about You, God, You will never forget about man.*

NOTES

1. Brueggemann, *New Cambridge Bible Commentary*, 80.

2. Charles Spurgeon, *The Treasury of David*, "Psalm 14, Title," https://archive.spurgeon.org/treasury/treasury.php.

3. Saint Robert Bellarmine, *A Commentary on the Book of Psalms*, 62.

4. Spurgeon, *The Treasury of David*, "Psalm 14, verse 3."

5. David Guzik, "Psalm 14: Fallen Man and a Faithful God," The Enduring Word Bible Commentary, https://enduringword.com/bible-commentary/psalm-14.

Week 3

Day 15

Walk This Way, Talk This Way, Live This Way

Who will dwell in Your holy hill? He who walks uprightly,
and does righteousness, and speaks truth in his heart.
—Psalm 15:1-2

Wow! Psalm 15. We have reached the halfway point in *30 Days of Praying the Psalms*. This is amazing. Can you think back to Psalm 1 and walk through each psalm remembering the keys from each chapter? Have you been using them? The best time to start using these keys is right when you are finished reading the chapter. Don't wait until you have read the entire book. Let me encourage you to pick up these keys the minute you have finished each chapter. Start using them right away, because it is almost like the previous psalms have laid a secure, steady foundation to build upon as we continue to walk through each chapter.

Here we are in Psalm 15. It starts with a question and ends with a promise, with the whole middle portion giving us directions on how to live in and host His presence. I love how *The Message* Bible says, "God, who gets invited to dinner at your place? How do we get on your guest list?" David asks the Lord, "Who can dwell with You, God? Who can remain or continually stay in Your presence? Who can be Your guest, having Your care and protection? Who can tarry or gather themselves together in God's dwelling, in Your home or in Your habitation?" (Strong's H7931). What a question! Oh God, let this be me. I want to be this one. I want to be the guest invited into Your presence.

With this very first question in Psalm 15, here lies our first key—*longing*. Can we start Psalm 15 by asking the Lord to stir up this kind of *longing* within us? Throughout David's entire life, he had an unquenchable hunger—this desire and need to be in the presence of the Lord. David prays a similar prayer in Psalm 42:1: "As the deer pants [or needs or yearns] for streams of water, so my soul pants [longs] for you, my God. ...When can I go and meet with God?" (NIV). May this hunger—this longing and desire that David had to continually be with God, to be in His presence—may it overflow within us as a continual hosting of His presence wherever we go. "Eternal One, who is invited to stay in Your dwelling? Who is granted passage to Your holy mountain?" (Ps. 15:1 VOICE).

One thing to remember when reading Psalm 15 is that David wrote this psalm with a future hope of Messiah while walking out the Old Covenant. However, today we are reading Psalm 15 through the lens of the New Covenant, knowing that Messiah has come—He lived, He died, and He rose again for us. He is the once and for all perfect sacrifice for all mankind, whose death caused the veil to rip in two—once and for all being our door and our way to come directly to God.

> *For God so loved the world that He gave His only begotten Son, that whoever believes in Him should not perish, but have eternal life. For God did not send His Son into the world to condemn the world, but that the world through Him might be saved* (John 3:16-17).

We pray Psalm 15 through the lens of John 3. We as believers can have a continual fellowship with God through praying His Word, singing His Word, talking to God through His Word. This, along with the empowerment of the Holy Spirit in our lives, stirs within us a continual longing for His presence. This is where I want to live and stay in the presence of God.

We use this key called *longing* by asking God the same question that David asked: "God, who can dwell in Your presence? God, can I dwell on Your holy hill? Can I be in the middle of Your set-apart presence?" If we can keep this key close and use it every single day, this key will help us to walk out verse 2, where David begins to list the qualifications of the one who can continually dwell in or host the presence of the Lord. David writes, "He who walks uprightly." He who lives perfect, whole, upright in conduct, and he who is altogether given to God. This altogether givenness is *in* the place where no eyes of man will ever see. This is the place of, "It's just You and me alone, God."

Walking uprightly is not just in public. It is *mostly* behind the scenes, where no one's eyes will never ever see; however, God's eyes see everything. This is the place where God desires and requires our walking uprightly, making choices for righteousness when the eyes of man will never see yet the gaze of God never leaves. It is the place where we are empowered by the Holy Spirit. The Holy Spirit empowers us to live and make good choices before God in the secret places of our life. This is God's delight and pleasure to help us walk uprightly.

Right here, we need some input from one of my favorites, David Guzik, who writes:

> David's principle is also accurate under the New Covenant in this sense: the conduct of one's life is a *reflection* of his fellowship with God. As John wrote: *If we say that we have fellowship with Him, and walk in darkness, we lie and do not practice the truth* (1 John 1:6). We might say that under the Old Covenant a righteous walk was the *precondition* for fellowship with God; under the New Covenant a righteous walk is the *result* of fellowship with God, founded on faith.[1]

As we pray through these verses, this key called *longing* will help us to walk uprightly, and it will help us to walk in righteousness; it will keep us on a straight path. This *longing* to be in the presence of the Lord—once you have felt this presence, there is nothing like it, and the longing only grows to host His presence continually. It will help us walk righteous in government and be right in speech or be the one who lives ethically right. We cannot fake truth and honesty. We cannot fake making good choices before God when no one is looking. But this key, this key called *longing*, it will keep us in the center, in the very presence of God as we walk out this psalm empowered by the Holy Spirit as we pray the Word of God.

Our second key for Psalm 15 is *speak truth*. As we pick up this key, we are reminded to speak truth out of the *deep places of our heart*. Our words and what we speak release life or death. Our words can draw us closer to the Lord or quickly quench the Spirit of the Lord in our lives. Psalm 15 shows us there is a direct correlation between dwelling in the presence of the Lord and our ability to control our tongue and what we say. This is the very thing that can keep us at a distance from the presence of the Lord.

The Book of James makes is very clear how dangerous our tongues can be: "For if we could control our tongues, we would be perfect and could also control ourselves in every other way" (James 3:2 NLT). In verse 6, James writes, "Among all the parts of the body, the tongue is a flame of fire. It is a whole world of wickedness, corrupting your entire body" (NLT).

We find David writing in Psalm 141:3, "Set a guard, O Lord, over my mouth; keep watch over the door of my lips." *The Voice Bible* says that same Scripture this way: "Guard my mouth, O Eternal One; control what I say. Keep a careful watch on every word I speak." Proverbs 25:23 out of *The Passion Translation* tells us, "As the north wind brings a storm, saying things you shouldn't brings a storm to any relationship."

So we could say, this second key, *speak truth*, should remind us of the power of our words or our tongue. James 1:26 says, "If you claim to be religious but don't control your tongue, you are fooling yourself, and your religion is worthless" (NLT).

This is a huge key that we must use minute by minute. We don't ever put this key down. For how we speak, what we say can directly affect our proximity to His presence. Spurgeon writes, "Some men's tongues bite more than their teeth. The tongue is not steel, but it cuts, and its wounds are very hard to heal; its worst wounds are not with its edge to our face, but with its back when our head is turned."[2] Ouch! This key provides us with a big heads-up. To use this key is simply to pray these Scriptures and ask the Holy Spirit to help us as we speak truth out of the deep places of our heart. It invites the Holy Spirit to guard and watch our words. He will help us. He will convict us, and this conviction is a beautiful thing. "Just don't say it. Put a cork in it." I literally carry a cork in my purse to remind myself—just don't say it. Don't be the spark that starts the whole forest on fire. I believe that it is the Lord's joy to help us, but we need to keep this key close so our words don't keep us at a distance from the presence that we so earnestly desire.

If we will just start with the little, start with saying yes to *longing*, then let that lead us to the cry of, "God, I want to *dwell in Your presence*." Whatever it looks like, say *yes*. This key, *longing*, will overflow in our lives and empower us by His Holy Spirit to do righteousness. In the comfort of our own home, we can and will be empowered as we pick up this key from Psalm 15 and then pick up the second key—*speak truth*.

Can you imagine? To live a more righteousness life in *secret*, not just in public but when no one is looking except the gaze of God. This is our incredible promise if we can simply use these keys. For these keys will lead us straight through this psalm, making good choices as we allow the Holy Spirit to set a guard on our lips in every season of our lives. *Longing* and *speak truth*.

DAILY PRAYER

Oh Lord, who can come into Your holy presence? Who can host Your beautiful presence continually? God, this is where I want to be. I want to be in Your holy presence Lord. I want to be with You, closer and closer.

Oh God, You have laid it out so clearly. You have written down the instructions. Lord, help me to walk down this path and to follow Your beautiful ways. Help my walk to be blameless and help me do what is righteous. Help me, Lord, to speak the truth out of the deep places of my heart.

Oh Lord, to have a blameless life and to do what is right! Help me to walk in truth without spot or blemish. Help me to walk uprightly. If I follow these instructions, if I walk with the help and grace of the Holy Spirit—oh Lord, Your promise to me is that I will stand. I will stand firm forever. I will not be shaken. I will not be prone to falling or slipping if I would follow Your leading and just walk this way and talk this way.

Help me, oh God. I want to host Your presence. I want to live in Your presence, God. To abide in Your presence, in Your beauty, in Your holiness.

Day 15: Write out Psalm 15

- Pray these verses out loud.
- Listen to the soaking for Psalm 15.
- Use these verses to talk to God.
- Can you remember the keys from this psalm?

Walk this way, talk this way, love this way, live this way.

NOTES

1. David Guzik, "Psalm 15: The Character of the One God Receives," The Enduring Word Bible Commentary, https://enduringword.com/bible-commentary/psalm-15.

2. Charles Spurgeon, *The Treasury of David*, "Psalm 15, verse 3," https://archive.spurgeon.org/treasury/treasury.php.

Day 16

The Excellent Ones

Keep me safe, my God, for in you I take refuge.
—Psalm 16:1 NIV

I say to the Lord, you are my Lord, you are my only good.
—Psalm 16:2 NABRE

*As for the saints (godly people) who are in the land, they are
the majestic and the noble and the excellent ones in
whom is all my delight.*
—Psalm 16:3 AMP

Psalm 16 is a psalm that one could actually write an entire book upon. There is so much in this incredible psalm. I only would like to focus on the first three verses and make these verses very personal in our journey through these first thirty psalms. The New Cambridge Bible Commentary writes, "Psalm 16 is a prayer to YHWH and an expression of confidence in YHWH's protection and provision for life."[1]

Have you ever been in a situation where you needed to be rescued, you needed someone to reach in or reach down and pluck you out of your trouble? This is where we find David in Psalm 16. He needed help. He needed a rescue, and the cry in David's heart was one in which he realized his only hope of deliverance was the hand of God. He did not trust in the cave that could hide him. He could not trust in his weapon or his shield that could protect him. His only help and hope was the Lord. His sole confidence was in the God of Jacob. This is our first key for Psalm 16—*God is my only help*. There is only One whom we can put every ounce of our hope into, and it is not in things or places, but it is only in the Lord. David understood this, and this is our key in Psalm 16. *God is my only help*.

I can remember a time when I was in Pemba, Mozambique visiting my friend Heidi Baker. Every Thursday her team heads out to many different places for outreach. We all loaded up in her big stick-shift truck, which Heidi drove amazingly. We drove far back into the bush-bush; I think we drove about four hours back into a place where few vehicles had driven. Much of this was a dirt road with big potholes, and we sang most of the way. Heidi showed the Jesus movie, and it's always translated into the local dialect of every people group so they are blessed to hear the whole story of the Gospel in their native tongue, and then Heidi gets up to preach and share the Gospel. This was an incredible meeting in the bush-bush. There was worship, there was the Jesus movie, there were healings, and I was so blessed to be in the middle of every bit of it.

When the meeting was over, I joined my friend Shara and one other girl, Whitney, as they were headed back to our tents. It was quite a walk back to where we had set up our tents. Shara said, "Follow me because I know where we are." As we began to follow our friend, we saw a light in the distance, which we all assumed was our camp. The closer we got to this light, we realized very quickly this was not our campsite. In fact, we didn't know who or what this campsite was, but it did not feel safe. My friend Shara, with urgency in her voice, said, "Turn out your lights and *run*" in a whisper that had "emergency" on the word *run*. So we turn all of our flashlights off, it is pitch black, and we are running with our arms linked away from this light that is not our camp, and we are running straight into the pitch black of the night. There is no moon to guide us in this black, dark night. There are no stars in the sky—only black darkness as we are running into trees, bushes, and branches as our lights are off. Where were we running? We did not know. We were hoping that we were running to something, yet we were just headed into the pitch blackness of the bush-bush.

This is not a safe place to be when you are in the bush-bush. One does not want to get lost in the bush-bush. We didn't see another light. We only saw black. It was dark and we did not see our camp. We began to cry out to the only One who could help us. We began to ask the Lord, "Help. Help. Help. We are in need of You, oh God. We are in need of You, We need You to reach down and direct us out of this dark blackness and guide us to our camp."

I don't know if you have ever been in a place that was not the safest to be and then on top of that to actually be lost in total darkness, but this is where I found myself on my very first trip to Pemba. Out in the middle of darkness, we needed a refuge, and the only refuge was God. We could not rely on our flashlights or our great sense of direction, for it was pitch black. We needed God to direct our steps and send out His light. We had no compass, no map, and we were not in a safe place. We needed that key—*God is my only help*. I don't remember how long we ran with arms linked in the pitch blackness of night, but in the middle of our cries—suddenly we saw a familiar light and camp. I don't know if the Lord reached down His beautiful hand and picked us up and put us in the right place with the right light; all I know is that suddenly we were in the place we needed to be.

This key has helped me walk through very emotional seasons, like the years and years of praying for my mom and her addiction to alcohol. This key helped me stay steady and engaged with the Lord when I had identical twins along with a two-year-old son. I still remember that season of getting no sleep, lots of tears, and yet pulling out that key of *God is my only help*. He surely was during that season. Then, many years later, when our youngest son was married and moved out—suddenly I found myself with an empty nest. Those same tears that I cried long ago rolled down my cheeks as the silence in our house and the loneliness that I felt were at times so hard. I would pull out that key, *God is my only help*. Yes, He was, and He still is.

This key, *God is my only help,* will never let us down. It is our assurance that God is with us. God is for us and God will always help us. He is our refuge and our safe place. He is our safest place. You may not find yourself in the middle of the bush-bush in Pemba needing a refuge and needing a light for your path—but wherever you are in life, this key will help you in everything you will ever face. *God is my only help*—this key will always provide strength and direction in our lives.

This prayer that David prayed started with a cry of *preserve me or help me or keep me safe, oh God*. Spurgeon expounds on this:

> "*Preserve me,*" keep, *or save me,* or as Horsley thinks, "*guard me,*" even as bodyguards surround their monarch, or as shepherds

protect their flocks. ...Thou art my great overshadowing Protector, and I have taken refuge beneath thy strength.[2]

This is our amazing God, and this is how He watches and guards us all throughout our lives. Keep this key close—*God is my only help.* When we need the saving strength of our God to reach down and pluck us out of the turbulent waters that life has thrown us into, this key, *God is my only help,* will keep our hearts focused on the only One who can and will help us.

There is one more key in these first couple of verses that has changed how I view myself before God: "As for the saints (godly people) who are in the land."[3] These saints are you and I. The saints are the ones who have set their hearts to love Jesus and follow His Word instead of following the world. We are the set-apart ones. We are the ones who live for Him while on the earth. We choose to be set apart for the purposes of God while we live on this earth, and God says to us through Psalm 16, "To the saints, set apart on the earth, to the one who gives all to the Lord."

This is you. This is me. And God continues and says: "They are the majestic and the noble and the excellent ones in whom is all my delight."[4] He who knows them best says of them, "in whom is all my delight." He says we are the great ones in the earth, the majestic ones, the noble ones. He has made us great. This last part is our key—*in whom is all my delight.*

When we bring in the Greek, "To the holy (ones) who (live) in His land, He (God) makes (them) marvels in whom (are) all of His pleasure." Have you ever thought of yourself in this manner? God makes us marvels, wonders, prodigies who do His will on the earth and we are God's delight. He delights in us and He calls us the noble ones, the excellent ones.

This knowledge of how God feels about us will cause us to live differently when no one is looking. This key, *in whom is all my delight*—oh, we need to hold this key close. Maybe get duplicate keys made and hang them on your mirror, hang them on your doorknob. Put them by your computer, hang one in your kitchen. Hold this key up in everything you do. Say this out loud. The more you say it, the more you will become it as our words are so powerful and this is the truth of who God says you and I are before Him. We are His delight. *Strong's Concordance* unwraps this word *delight* as "pleasure, a valuable thing, acceptable, things desired" (Strong's H2656). Oh, do you see your incredible value before God?

Spurgeon says of these saints, "They are his Hephzibah and his land Beulah, and before all worlds his delights were with these chosen sons of men."[5] All of God's joy is in these set-apart saints. Oh, what amazing keys in the first couple of verses. Take these with you everywhere you go. Say them out loud. *God is my only help* and *in whom is all my delight*. Both of these keys together will empower your heart in every single crisis you might find yourself in. They will encourage you in the hard times and keep the heart alive in the dry seasons.

DAILY PRAYER

Keep me safe, oh God. Watch over me and guard, hold me in Your heart and keep me in Your thoughts. Lord, I run to You, my refuge and my hope. You keep me close. You protect me under Your shadow. You are watching over me. You are the ever-watching One. You keep me in Your steady gaze.

Oh, my soul will sing to the Lord, "You are my God. You are my only good." My soul will say to the Lord, "The only good thing inside of me is You. You are my maker, my mediator."

Can you imagine Heaven singing this song over us? To the saints, set apart on the earth, to the ones who give all to the Lord, can you hear the song of Heaven? All My desire, all my delight is in these ones, set apart. These are My excellent ones, the noble, the mighty, the glorious ones.

Even Your correction tenderly makes me want to praise You. Your whispers in the night give me wisdom, giving me counsel even as I sleep, showing me what to do. Even in my sleep, in the night, You give me counsel—in my dreams.

I have You ever before me. I will not be shaken; I will not be moved. My eyes are always on You. You are so very close to me; my confidence will never be shaken.

Day 16: Write out Psalm 16

- Pray these verses out loud.

- Listen to the soaking for Psalm 16.

- Use these verses to talk to God.

- Can you remember the keys from this psalm?

> *These are my excellent ones and they fulfill all My desires.*

NOTES

1. Brueggemann, *New Cambridge Bible Commentary*, 87.

2. Charles Spurgeon, *The Treasury of David*, "Psalm 16, verse 1," https://archive.spurgeon.org/treasury/treasury.php.

3. Psalm 16:2 AMP.

4. Psalm 16:2 AMP.

5. Spurgeon, *The Treasury of David*, "Psalm 16, verse 3."

Day 17

Nighttime Visitations

O Lord, hear my plea for justice. Listen to my cry for help.
Pay attention to my prayer...You have tested my thoughts
and examined my heart in the night.
—Psalm 17:1,3 NLT

For in a visitation of the night you inspected my heart and refined
my soul in fire until nothing vile was found in me.
—Psalm 17:3 TPT

Have you ever considered that one of the most opportune times for God to encounter the human heart, soul, and inner man is while we are sleeping? Think about it—God comes as a refining fire, burning away things we don't really need and speaking truth to all of the troubled places in our heart and soul. And while we are sleeping we cannot say anything like, "Yes, but...."

Many have been visited in the night by the promise of the all-consuming fire who looks over and inspects, who refines and speaks truth. We are literally changed through nighttime visitations. Do you know that Psalm 17 promises each of us these unexpected encounters? All we do is go to sleep—even right there the consuming fire is working, refining, speaking truth, and highlighting to us what God is doing in our life. He is just that good. He is busy at work within us even while we sleep.

Psalm 17 gives us a cry for justice but also a promise of visitation. Spurgeon calls this psalm "An appeal to Heaven from the persecutions of earth" and writes of David, "He that has the worst cause makes the most noise."[1] We might say, "The squeaky wheel gets the oil," meaning the loudest sound gets the most attention—it gets the oil and it gets the oil quickly. In this psalm, David states the very same cry three different ways. It is as if he is wanting God to feel the pull as he cries aloud for help and keeps on crying out and keeps on crying out. David prays *hear, listen,* and *pay attention*, God.

Now, this is our first key in Psalm 17—*hear, listen, pay attention*. It is a continual, repetitive cry to God—to the only one who can grant David justice before all of his enemies, before those who were with David, and before those who were against him. This is an important key for us to carry because, just like God came through for David, He will come through for us. He is the only One who can grant you and I justice before any accusations we may face in life. It is a lesson for us to learn and to cry out and turn to God as our only hope and help when finding ourselves in similar accusations. When we cry out for justice, let us hope in God alone, just like David did. In *The Enduring Word* online commentary, David Guzik writes, "This was an important way that David left his problem to the Lord. 'God, I refuse to take matters into my own hands. I will wait for *vindication* to *come from Your presence*; I want to know that this is Your work and not mine.'"[2]

This key gives us this repetition, this continual cry for justice that I can almost hear David's voice grow more intense with a deeper groan from deep within him as he begins to cry to the Lord. When we look up these words, which happen to be our first key for Psalm 17, we will find that all three words basically mean the same thing. So David was saying the same thing in three different ways. As we unwrap these three words, they actually entwine themselves together, meaning the same thing prayed in the same way, but the sound of the cry may get louder and more intense with each phrase. When David prays, "Hear my cry," it is like that is just not enough, so he says the same thing using a little different verbiage, "Listen," and after that still David moves onward with "Pay attention."

When we unwrap the word *hear*, it can mean "listen, give me Your attention." (Strong's H8085). What I love about this word *hear* is that it is the same word from Deuteronomy 6:4-5 when God begins to tell Israel, "Hear, O Israel." Right here, God is crying out from Heaven to Israel, "Hey, hear these words, listen up and pay attention." This word is more than just hearing or listening or paying attention, but it actually means to *follow through*. It is not just "hearing" but it also includes the follow through—that there is obedience connected to the hearing. God is crying out to Israel, "Hear and obey Israel. Don't just listen and let the words fall to the ground but actually do and set these words into motion in your life. Change your life so you are obeying what you hear Me saying." In Deuteronomy 6, God is talking to Israel, but in Psalm 17, David is using this same word in talking to God, meaning, "God, listen, pay attention, and answer this plea."

Maybe he was thinking and meditating on Deuteronomy 6? Maybe David was singing in his meditations from this chapter, remembering God's cry to Israel when He said *hear*. David would have understood the meaning of this word to hear and listen and actually do this in your life. So with this cry for justice, David turned to the only One who could totally bring justice and truth to the accusations he found himself surrounded with. There was only One who could settle everything, for God understood the motives and actions of David just as He also knew and understood the motives and actions of David's enemies. The *New Cambridge Bible Commentary* writes, "Any vindication will come from the divine judge, for YHWH is the one that sees to the core character of both the psalmist and the enemies."[3] God was the just Judge who could and would bring about total acquittal for David. This is such an important key—*hear, listen, and pay attention.* It is learning the art of supplication without growing weary should the answer tarry.

> David would not have been a man after God's own heart, if he had not been a man of prayer. He was a master in the sacred art of supplication. He flies to prayer in all times of need, as a pilot speeds to the harbour in the stress of tempest.[4]

This plea for justice leads us right to the promise of nighttime visitations. This is our second key for Psalm 17—*visitation.* It is as if this cry for justice invites the Refiner's fire to come in the midst of the night. This is the easy part, for all we do is go to sleep. The Lord is like an inspector—He investigates, He examines, He comes when we are sleeping. In our sleep, the Refiner comes and He visits us. He looks and inspects our heart, our soul, our thoughts. He is inspecting and He is looking closely. If He finds anything contrary to light, He gets out His Refiner's fire rod and burns it away. Can you imagine? Night after night, all we do is go to sleep and the Refiner Himself comes into our room; He begins to inspect our secret of secrets, our deepest thoughts, our words, our heart. Should He find anything that looks opposite of light, He refines right then. Night after night, He comes and He continues to look, observe, and refine until He finds nothing—until He finds nothing at all that is wicked or vile within us. He continues these nighttime visitations until there is nothing within us that is darkness. He comes again and again until we look like Him.

The word here for *visit* can mean "deposit, to oversee, to give oversight" (Strong's H6485). He comes, the Refiner's fire, He comes to make a deposit of Himself. He comes to give oversight in our ever-growing relationship with Him on our journey to become more like Him. He comes to purge away or melt that which is darkness. He comes to make us pure, to oversee us as we become more and more in His image. As we truly become His image bearers on the earth.

In the Greek, both verbs *proved* and *visited* reinforce the idea of testing, reviewing, and assessing. Just as a worthwhile teacher fairly grades tests from their students or a cadre challenges soldiers for selection, so God is described here as a rigorous judge of character and commitment for His people—even when they're sleeping.[5]

So we need to keep hold of these keys. Our key of *hear, listen, and pay attention* reminds us that God does hear our plea, and He responds to our cries with an answer. His answer to our cries is His Refiner's fire. This is our second key—*visitations*. We have a promise that when we cry out, He comes when we sleep, and in this nighttime visit He removes all that does not look like Himself until we truly can arise in the morning dawn hours saying, "When I awake, I awake in Your likeness and I am satisfied."

DAILY PRAYER

Hear my plea for justice, listen to my cry for help. Pay attention to my prayer, for it comes from honest lips, O God. Let my cry arise to You.

Declare me innocent, declare me righteous, for You see everything in me. You know what I did. You know what I didn't do. You have tested my thoughts, examined my heart in the night. In a visitation of the night, You inspected my heart, refined my soul in the fire. All I do is go to sleep and even right there You are working on me. Even right there You try my heart. You refine me in the fire.

You inspect my heart, O God, until You find nothing at all that is contrary to You. There Your fire meets me, Your fire purifies. So show me Your unfailing love and show me Your wonderful ways. Show me and keep me, as the apple of Your eye, and guard me like You would Your very own eye and hide me in the shadow of Your wings. I feel so near, I feel so close, I feel so safe right here in the shadow of Your wings.

Day 17: Write out Psalm 17

- Pray these verses out loud.

- Listen to the soaking for Psalm 17.

- Use these verses to talk to God.

- Can you remember the keys from this psalm?

I will be satisfied, God. I will be satisfied in Your glory, in Your likeness.

NOTES

1. Charles Spurgeon, *The Treasury of David*, "Psalm 17, Title and Subject, verse 1," https://archive.spurgeon.org/treasury/treasury.php.

2. David Guzik, "Psalm 17: Shelter under the Shadow of His Wings," The Enduring Word Bible Commentary, https://enduringword.com/bible-commentary/psalm-17.

3. Brueggemann, *New Cambridge Bible Commentary*, 90.

4. Charles Spurgeon, *The Treasury of David*, "Psalm 17, Title and Subject," https://archive.spurgeon.org/treasury/treasury.php.

5. Joseph Meyer, formerly a Doctoral Fellow in Classical Languages and Literature at UCSB.

Day 18

Servanthood: A Love Song and Delight

A psalm of David, the servant of the Lord. He sang this song to the Lord on the day the Lord rescued him from all his enemies and from Saul. He sang: I love you, Lord; You are my strength. The Lord is my rock, my fortress, and my savior; my God is my rock, in whom I find protection. He is my shield, the power that saves me, and my place of safety. ...He rescued me because he delights in me.
—Psalm 18:1-2,19 NLT

Have you ever asked the question, "God, what does it look like for You to answer our cries? Do You personally answer every prayer or send out Your angels?" If you have ever asked yourself these questions, this is your psalm. David writes in detail what it looks like when our tiny prayers arise to God and then God's response back. He reveals to us how God comes down *to us*. He is a God of action. He shows us what God looks like and how God feels when He comes for our rescue. The whole deliverance is written line by line in Psalm 18:4-19. He wrote it down for our benefit so we could see the actions of God at the sound of our cries.

Sometimes I wonder if Psalm 18 follows the great storyline of answered prayer. I think of Jacob in Genesis 28 when he encountered God at the place he called Bethel, the Gateway of Heaven. Jacob saw a ladder from earth to Heaven going straight up into the sky, with God Almighty at the very top. Angels were descending and ascending in this great vision called *Jacob's ladder*. Jacob saw God at the very top of the ladder. Jacob saw the One making all of the decrees and decisions from the very top. God is the rule maker. He governs the entire earth. Jacob saw the true governmental center of the whole universe. He saw it in the heavens with God at the very top.

Fast forward to Psalm 18, where David writes of his great thankfulness to God for all of God's mighty rescues in his life. David does what every great writer does. He pulls out his pen to describe the cry that reaches God's ear. It is as if he could see his cry arise and land in the heart of God. Then, he writes a detailed account of what God does *when* He answers. And I believe this is the same way God responds to us and answers our cry.

Maybe we could say Psalm 18 is a written account of our God, seated on the throne, hearing our cries, and then He comes down to our rescue filled with a righteous anger for His beloved ones. He comes as the great deliverer. This psalm could actually be an incredible movie or art series. If you are an artist, please paint this chapter. David Guzik writes:

> This psalm is virtually the same as the psalm sung by David at the very end of his life, as recorded in 2 Samuel 22. It is likely that David composed this song as a younger man; yet in his

old age David could look back with great gratitude and sing this song again, looking at his whole life.[1]

The title portion of this psalm tells us who wrote the psalm, *why* he wrote the psalm, and *when* he wrote it. This part of the psalm is not just a title but holds some important information about David. At this point in time, David is king, but he does not mention his royalty. It is almost as if he is writing of his greatest pleasure, and that is *being a servant* of the Most High. Can you even imagine that? He is king. He has great favor. He is the sweet psalmist of Israel, and yet he writes his name in the title: "A psalm of David, the *servant of the Lord*." Spurgeon writes, "David...makes no mention of his royalty; hence we gather that he counted it a higher honour to be the Lord's servant than to be Judah's king."[2]

This is our first key. It is right in the middle of the title—*the servant of the Lord*. He penned forever and all through eternity a psalm of David, the *servant of the Lord*. This word *servant* or *bondservant* is taken from a word that means "to serve, to work, to become a servant." It also means "worshiper" (Strong's H5647). Now, a bondservant is a person bound in service without wages. It is someone who can leave and be free but chooses to stay out of loyalty and service.

Right here at the beginning of this great encounter with the Lord, David shows us his heart to serve. This is a crucial key for every believer's walk in God. It is not a lower thing; it is actually the highest thing. John 13 shows us the very heart of Jesus right before He went to the cross. He did not just talk about serving; He actually gave each disciple a picture of serving by dressing like a servant as He began to wash their feet. This is His heart's posture. And continually throughout the Psalms, David called himself *servant,* showing us that it was not beneath David to call himself a servant—but it was his joy and passion to serve the Lord. This is our key from Psalm 18—*servant.* If we can see ourselves the way that David saw himself, it is a worthy and beautiful title. Maybe David remembered how Moses called himself *servant of the Lord*; therefore, it became dear to his heart to wear that same title throughout his life. In the New Testament, Paul, James, Peter, and Jude, among many others, called themselves *servant of the Lord.* They used this very key as they set their hearts to serve the Lord in all His ways. Keep this key close, *servant of the Lord,* and use it daily. I believe it is an on-ramp for great encounters with God.

David starts the very first verse with "I love You." This is our second key for Psalm 18—*I love You.* Say these words all day long. We can never tell the Lord, "I love You" enough. This will keep our love for God alive even in the midst of the strongest winds and storms. The more you speak of your love for God, the more that love will grow and overflow. Then, David's love song begins to tell of who the Lord is and what He does. When we think of these descriptions, we actually have a word picture in our mind of who God is. David writes, "He is my rock." This is a rock like bedrock that has been set in place for generations, for thousands of years—a rock that is unmovable and unshakable (Strong's H5553). Everything can be shaking in our life, but God is our rock that does not move. God is our sure foundation.

David writes, "The Lord is my fortress." A fortress is a place of safety where enemies cannot follow or reach. God does the same today for us. David begins to describe God in military terms to paint the picture in our minds that God is a warrior who fights for us and with us. He never changes. This amazing warrior David describes in great detail is also the one who fights for us. Derek Kidner writes, "In this rush of metaphors David re-lives his escapes and victories...and probes into their meaning. 'The *rock,* or cliff where he had been so unexpectedly delivered from Saul...the stronghold.'"[3] What is amazing is that David starts this psalm with a love song. He starts with his great love for God and then goes right onto the battlefield with the warrior who provides a safe and steady place for David. Pray Psalm 18 with the inscription that David wrote using these two keys, *servant of the Lord,* then going right into a love song—Lord, *I love You.*

I believe that these two keys are the on-ramp to great encounters with God. For David then begins to detail the most amazing encounter where he sees what it looks like for God to come down and save. David writes what God looks like with a zeal for His people. He reveals to us the God who loves to set us free from every hindrance and from every battle that the enemy would try to wage. David writes and describes what God looks like in His righteous anger. He writes down what God does, how God fights, and how God is God over man, creation, time, and circumstances.

This great poetic scene in verses 4-19 is describing God the champion warrior who comes down for David's dramatic rescue. When there was no way of escape, when there was no way out of the battle, God made His grand appearance and became David's great escape.

This leads us to our third key in Psalm 18 from verse 19, where David writes: "He delivered me because He delighted in me." This key I am calling *delights.* Oh, this is a wonderful reality of our God. He does not just deliver because He can; He does not reach down and pluck us out of trouble because He is able. He comes to our rescue because He delights in us. Our voice is pleasing to Him. He loves our sound. He takes great joy in being the One who delivers us—even if it is continually. This is an important key—*delights*. It's something our heart needs to say and sing over and over—we have a God who delights to deliver.

This word *delivers* means "incline, to bend, to be pleased with, desire, have favor, have pleasure" (Strong's H2654). Can you picture our God who has such a desire and pleasure over His beloved ones that He goes out of His way, He bends down to us, He comes down to where we are and rescues. He saves, He delivers, not because He has to but because He desires to rescue us with pleasure in His heart.

When we bring in the Greek, *delivered* is a verb that frequently describes the actions of God who rescues someone in need. *Delighted* has a unique meaning, when used in the Septuagint, different from its typical definition in classical Greek. Typically, it refers to someone's will or intent to complete a task, yet here it means to delight in someone. In this case, it is the faithful.[4]

Let this be the picture in your heart every single time you read and pray through the Word of God. He delights in you; you give Him great pleasure; therefore, He bends down to your rescue. Oh beloved, these are simple and necessary keys that I believe will lead us to a great encounter in which the Holy Spirit will bring us on an amazing journey where we see the Lord on His great mission to deliver us. Then pull out the last key in Psalm 18, *delights*, and know that God does all of this because He simply *delights*.

DAILY PRAYER

Psalm 18, a psalm of David, the servant of the Lord—I want that title for my very own also. Show me the beauty in serving. It is powerful before You. Oh Lord, let this be my signature—servant of the Lord.

I will love You, oh Lord my strength. You are my help, and with my whole heart, Lord, with all my devotion, I will love You. You are my rock. You are my sure foundation. You are my fortress. You are my strength in whom I trust. You lift me high above all of the chaos and You, God, delight in me.

When everything is shaken all around me, You are my rock and I'll stay with You. This rock is my sure foundation; it keeps me steady all through the shaking. I love You, God. You delight to save me. Lord. I'll call upon Your name. You are worthy of all praise.

It's the song of a grateful heart overwhelmed with God. You deliver me over and over again simply because You love me. You delight in me.

Day 18: Write out Psalm 18

- Pray these verses out loud.
- Listen to the soaking for Psalm 18.
- Use these verses to talk to God.
- Can you remember the keys from this psalm?

You carry me away. You are my great escape. I'll stay right here with You.

NOTES

1. David Guzik, "Psalm 18: Great Praise from a Place of Great Victory," The Enduring Word Bible Commentary, https://enduringword.com/bible-commentary/psalm-18.

2. Spurgeon, *The Treasury of David*, "Psalm 18, Title," https://archive.spurgeon.org/treasury/treasury.php.

3. Kidner, Psalms, 108.

4. Joseph Meyer, formerly a Doctoral Fellow in Classical Languages and Literature at UCSB.

Day 19

The Prize
of a Lifetime

*The law of the Lord is perfect, converting the soul; the testimony of
the Lord is sure, making wise the simple; the statutes of the Lord
are right, rejoicing the heart; the commandment of the Lord is
pure, enlightening the eyes; the fear of the Lord is clean, enduring
forever; the judgments of the Lord are true and righteous altogether.
More to be desired are they than gold, yea, than much fine
gold; sweeter also than honey and the honeycomb.*
—Psalm 19:7-10 NKJV

Psalm 19 takes me back to my high school/college days living in my hometown of Wamego, Kansas. People think of Kansas and they think *flat*—as in, it is flat and boring. But Wamego is this little town surrounded by rolling hills, prairies, valleys, and a lot of good farmland. But most of all, my home is there. I grew up on the same farm that my dad grew up on. It was the same farm his mom grew up on. In the same way that Scarlet O'Hara loved her Tara, that is the same way I love our farm. If I was going through trouble, chaos, or emotional drama, my dad would call me and say, "Daughter, just come back to the farm for a couple of days."

I have a clear memory of being home from college and walking in the front door; my eyes were met with glistening lights and a Christmas tree full of sparkling tinsel and colorful ornaments. I gathered with some friends for a night of Christmas carols and we ended the evening with a simple worship song. I was a fairly new believer and didn't realize this worship song was word for word from the Psalms.

It was sometime later I began to ask the question: "What does this even mean? The Law of the Lord, the testimony, statutes, commandments? Are they alike? Are they different?" Now this is the beauty of singing the Psalms and singing the Scriptures—the minute I began to sing Psalm 19, these words came alive. We know from Hebrews 4:12 that the Word of God is alive and full of living power. So think about this—even though I did not understand what I was singing, these words from Psalm 19 were already working on my heart, soul, mind, and body. They were refreshing, restoring, converting, and enlightening, because that is what Psalm 19 says these words will do.

Here lies our first key for Psalm 19. This key is called *sing the Word*. Now, if this key has already made you a bit apprehensive, then start with saying and praying the Word out loud. As you gain confidence, try throwing in some melodies. This key will be very easy to use, because there is already a song from Psalm 19. This key, *sing the Word*, will work on every single psalm. In fact, it will work in every single Scripture. Get by yourself and just sing the Word out loud. God empowers us with His words even if we do not grasp the full meaning. They are restoring, renewing, healing, breaking off negative emotions, empowering us on the inside. Oh, the kindness of God who would make restoration, refreshing, and empowering so simple as we *sing the Word*. Sing it even before you understand the words, for understanding will come in the singing.

In Psalm 19, David reveals the power of the Word and what it actually does to us, for us, and within us. God is the master Creator, ever refining and molding our life. Paul says this so perfectly in Philippians 1:6: "I am confident of this very thing, that He who began a good work in you will perfect it until the day of Jesus Christ."

He is the one overseeing the work. The only way to walk through these verses is to believe and know that God is the ultimate author and finisher of it all. He is making sure these words have their perfect way and work in our life. Keep this key close as we walk through these next verses.

In this portion of Psalm 19, David writes in the poetic form of Hebrew parallelism, which is basically writing similar ideas over and over in different ways to add emphasis. It is not about rhyming but about writing similar ideas—the law of the Lord, the testimony, the precepts, the commandments, the commands, the statutes. In reading these verses, it was to produce great impact in the heart of the reader. It's as if David wanted to drive this point right into every heart—if we keep these, they actually will produce something within us.

Which brings us to the second key. I am calling this key *Word of God*. These are promises to live by every single day. You can pray these daily and they will never get old. I believe it is important for us to sing these out and know them clearly because these four verses are what the Word of God does within us. This is a powerful key to carry with you. David Guzik writes:

David then explains seven glorious statements about the word of God: how wonderful and effective it is. As is common in other places—especially the great Psalm 119—David used a variety of expressions to refer to the word of God (law, testimony, statutes, commandment, fear, judgments). It is best to see these as poetic terms describing God's written revelation in general, rather than one specific type of revelation (such as only the laws given in the Mosaic law).[1]

For this reason, as we walk through the following verses we are going to use one phrase to sum up all of these poetic terms—*the Word of God.*

David writes, "The Word of God is perfect." What does that mean? It is complete. It is entire. It is without blemish. It is flawless. It is whole and full, and it is healthful. There is nothing that is left out and nothing needs to be added. This Word converts the soul. It will refresh and rescue our soul. It will benefit and revive our soul. It will convert and repair our soul. It will cause the soul—the core of our emotions, our appetite, mind, desires, and passion—to be alive in the Word.

The Greek for the word *convert* is a verb that means to turn around, return, convert, repent. What is interesting here is that the verb is circumstantial. It could be translated simply as, "The law of the Lord is perfect and it corrects the soul," yet other options exist, such as, "When the law of the Lord converts the soul, it's perfect" or "Since the law of the Lord converts the soul, it's perfect." Perhaps the author of this psalm kept the language vague to imply that many of these options are relevant and useful to those who meditate upon His law day and night.[2]

The Word is sure. It is trustworthy. It is firm and permanent, and it is faithful. The Word will make the simple minded one become wise in mind, word, or act. The Word will teach wisdom. It will instruct us. The Word is reliable and true, instilling wisdom to open minds. We can be confident in this.

The Word of the Lord is right. It is straight; it is not a winding road with a dead end. It is a straight road that leads to life. The Word is correct. It is pleasing and straightforward. It is righteous, and to walk on this straight path will give us joy. The Word of God is so correct and straight that it *causes* our hearts to rejoice. It makes even our memory to be glad. It causes our will, our intellect, and our inner man to rejoice. What an incredible promise.

The Word of the Lord is pure. It is clear. It is clean. The Word enlightens us, and it will cause our face to shine. This word will lighten, it will brighten one's countenance. This Word will bring a lost soul back to life.

To love the Word and to revere this Word causes us to remain and endure through all seasons. It will keep us steady for the long road through the decades. No matter what anybody says, no matter how many social groups would come against the Word of God, this Word, will last forever. The Word of the Lord is reliable. It is firm, it is just, and each word is fair.

The Word of the Lord is true. It is established. It is our divine instruction. It is truth, stability—perpetually. This Word will cleanse our way. It can never ever be repealed. It is clean and it will make us clean. David puts such high praise on it that he says, "These are to be more desirable than gold." If the wealth of the world was offered to you or if you found yourself winning millions from the Publishers

Clearing House giveaway, David said these commands, the Law of the Lord, should be desired, longed for, and craved more than any financial gain or anything you could ever perceive yourself blessed with. More desirable than anything is His Word, His commands, His testimonies, His instructions. This is our prize of a lifetime. This is the prize we reach for.

David writes what he has found true in his own life. Then he invites us to run this race into desire for the Word of God and these testimonies and truths in this Word. They are to be more desirable than all the gold, but even more than gold, than the finest of refined gold. These words should be desirable, for this is the Word that revives. This is the word that heals. This is the Word that makes the whole person. It touches, heals, and empowers our whole body, soul, spirit, emotions, thoughts, and heart; it's this Word. This is the prize of a lifetime.

Here lies our third key. I am calling it *the prize*. This is our prize of a lifetime—that we could keep this powerful Word on our lips minute by minute. It is the greatest prize one could ever receive. To use this key is to keep these words alive day by day and to seek after them with all of our heart and all our devotion.

We can read of the wisest of men, but at the end of the day, it's this Word that enlightens; it's the Word that makes us whole. It is the Word that gives wisdom to our hearts, to our minds, and in this is a beautiful promise using these keys of *sing the Word* and *Word of God* and *the prize*. As you use these keys you will find your desires turning to the His Word. You will find desire for His Word spring up and you will find yourself crave it more than anything.

David says these words affect the human heart and mind. They are sweeter than honey and even sweeter than fresh honey that is dripping down the honeycomb. Take pleasure in this; take great delight in His Word. David Guzik writes:

> Sweeter also than honey and the honeycomb: For King David, God's word was not only to be held in greater esteem than material wealth, but also greater than experiences of the senses. Honey is sweet and pleasant to eat, but God's word is sweeter still.[3]

Pick up these three simple keys from Psalm 19—number one, *sing the Word*; number two, *Word of God*; number three, *the prize*. Sing so these words go into the inner man, and then hit the replay button so this song continues. If you cannot bring yourself to sing at first, then speak these verses out loud. Then grab key number two—know the life-giving power within the *Word of God*. These words need to be sung or spoken, not read silently. Then, key number three—the prize. This is the real prize to reach for. As you pick up these keys, watch all of the promises come alive and make you shine fair as the moon, bright as the sun, from the inside out.

DAILY PRAYER

Oh Lord, thank You for Your Word. May Your Word have its perfect work in my life. I will take Your Word and sing it out, I will say it loud that it would have its perfect work in my life.

Lord, Your Word is perfect in every single way; it revives my soul and it leads me to truth. It changes the simple to wise. Your words, Your commands, they make me joyful; they cause me to radiate and shine with a great light from the inside.

Your Word is pure; it challenges me to keep close. Oh Lord, thank You that Your Word brings joy, it brings gladness as I follow Your Word. It's perfect. It's forever and it remains the same. Your Word is constant; it's true. Your Word brings peace to my soul.

As I seek and go after Your Word, it keeps me on the right path. Your Word is a promise. It's a guarantee. If I follow Your Word, it's a pathway to success in this life. It's a gateway to You.

Oh Lord, help me to desire Your Word more than gold. Your Word is my prize. Your Word is the prize of a lifetime. To carry these words in my heart as I sing and pray Your Word—it revives my soul. Your Word leads me to truth. It leads me to You.

Lord, Your Word it is what I want. It's what I need, and it's what I cling to.

Day 19: Write out Psalm 19

- Pray these verses out loud.

- Listen to the soaking for Psalm 19.

- Use these verses to talk to God.

- Can you remember the keys from this psalm?

> *Lord, Your words, Your commandments, Your testimonies are Your instructions for life.*

NOTES

1. David Guzik, "Psalm 19: The Heavens, the Word, and the Glory of God," The Enduring Word Bible Commentary, https://enduringword.com/bible-commentary/psalm-19.

2. Joseph Meyer, formerly a Doctoral Fellow in Classical Languages and Literature at UCSB.

3. Guzik, "Psalm 19."

Day 20

Chariots and Horses

Now I know that the Lord saves His anointed; He will answer him
from His holy heaven with the saving strength of His right hand.
Some trust in chariots, and some in horses, but we will remember
the name of the Lord our God. They are brought down
and fallen, but we arise and stand upright.
—Psalm 20:6-8

I still remember the very first time I saw the old classic movie *Ben Hur* starring a young Charlton Heston. As a young teen, I remember sitting on the floor glued to the TV. I was very impacted by that great scene with the chariot races. My mom loved this movie, and I still have memories of the different scenes. If you have not seen this movie, the chariot scene alone will bring some clarity to Psalm 20. You can see the greatness of these chariots and the tools of warfare built into each chariot. You can see the ferocious strength of the horses. This scene was a chariot race, but the race was not only about winning but taking out your opponent. So you could say this race was a battle to live, a race to win. Now bring this movie into today and add the element of surround sound to that chariot race and the sound of the wheels of the chariots and the running of the horses. The sound is thunderous. Almost as if to portray a sound of victory.

This chariot race was forever bookmarked in my memories, so when I began to read Psalm 20, I immediately had that memory of years ago watching *Ben Hur*.

Of course, Psalm 20 is much more than a chariot race. This psalm shows the battle plans of victory that David wrote out and sang aloud. So if you are in the midst of a battle and you need a rescue, if you need battle plans—this is your psalm. Many feel that Psalms 20 and 21 go together, with Psalm 20 being the request and cry to God for deliverance as David heads into battle and Psalm 21 being a song of thanksgiving as David and his men return victorious to the city.

Psalm 20 is an anthem of war that the people would sing over David as he would go out to battle. They were asking for God to help David, to be his defense, and to strengthen him.

Here in verse 6, David has a response to the first five verses. His response was also to strengthen his own heart. He sings out, "Now I know that the Lord saves His anointed." David begins to give and sing out a response straight to God. He declares his unwavering confidence in the God of Jacob, singing that the God of Jacob will rescue and hear his cry. His song turns into a prophetic decree that God's mighty hands will save. And remember, this is before David has even got to the battle. He is singing and declaring the victory by the hand of mighty God before he has even seen the armies raging against him.

This is our first key—*I know the Lord saves His anointed*. This key has a longer title because it is of great importance that we are able to sing out and declare loud every part of these seven words.

I know...

This is the personal part. It is not just that *people* know God will save David, but David makes this confession *himself* in the battle anthem—*I know*. This is a huge key. We have to grasp this in the depths of our heart. Singing and praying these seven words over and over will cause these words to take root in our soul, our mind, our core, and our heart. This is a great invitation for you and for me to know, to understand, and to comprehend that it is God who saves *us*. God saves *me*. We need to use this key over and over. *I know*. What do we know?

I know that the Lord...

This is of great importance. It is not David's army or his wisdom or his incredible skill that saves him, but David gives credit to the Lord. It is the Eternal One; it is Yah. This is Jehovah, the name of the supreme God (Strong's H3068). Oh, this is such an important key for us. I know the Lord saves, He delivers, He saves in battle, He gives victory.

I know the Lord saves...

Who does He save? Beloved, He saves you. *I know*, I am convinced, I know in the depths of my heart, that the *Lord God*, the Eternal One, *He saves,* He delivers, He gives victory to *His anointed*—to me.

I know the Lord saves His anointed.

Who is His anointed? *It is you.* It is me. This is not the place to leave yourself out of the story, no matter how little the battle or no matter how big the warfare. It is where we put ourselves right in the middle. For God, His Word, is the same, yesterday, today, and forever. He remains. So the God who rescues and saves David also rescues and saves us. He saves you. He calls you His anointed one. This psalm is our psalm. We can use it to fight every single battle we face today. Keep this key close—*I know the Lord saves His anointed.*

David—quite possibly riding out from the city, listening and receiving the song the people were singing over him—began to write it all into song. This became his battle cry anthem when heading into battle. What I love about Psalm 20 is that he was agreeing with the prayers of the people and he began to declare and sing out the victory, reminding himself. As he headed toward the battle, he sang this song—possibly as a reminder to *not* look at the chariots and to *not* look at the strength of the horses or the multitude of them. He wanted to sing out and declare loud that he would put all of his trust in the name of the Lord his God.

Maybe David was thinking of Moses and the song of Moses when God was the great deliverer of the battle as Moses and his people were pinned between the army of Pharaoh and the Red Sea. God came through when there was no other way, and Moses sang out this song. Maybe as David began to ride toward his battles, he began to think of all of the times the God of Jacob rescued and gave victory to the patriarchs of old. So he put his trust in God Almighty more than what his eyes would actually see.

In the *Treasury of David*, Spurgeon writes:

Chariots and horses make an imposing show, and with their rattling, and dust, and fine caparisons [which is rich decorative coverings], make so great a figure that vain man is much taken with them; yet the discerning eye of faith sees more in an invisible God than in all these. The most dreaded war-engine of David's day was the war-chariot, armed with scythes [which is a with a long curved blade at the end of a long pole attached to which are one or two short handles], which mowed down men like grass: this was the boast and glory of the neighbouring nations; but the saints considered the name of Jehovah to be a far better defense. As the Israelites might not keep horses, it was natural for them to regard the enemy's cavalry with more than usual dread. It is, therefore, all the greater evidence of faith that the bold songster can here disdain even the horse of Egypt in comparison with the Lord of hosts.[1]

So David sings out and reminds himself to not just look with his eyes because his deliverance comes from God. Do not look at the strength of the horses nor the multitude of chariots or the vast army before him—do not look with your eyes—but trust in the name. Trust in the name of the God who came through and rescued and delivered Jacob. This is our second key—*remember the name of the God of Jacob.*

Our trust can never be in the strength of people or things, it must always be in the name of the God of Jacob. Spurgeon writes:

"Our God" in covenant, who has chosen us and whom we have chosen; this God is our God. The name of our God is JEHOVAH, and this should never be forgotten; the self-existent, independent, immutable, ever-present, all-filling I AM.[2]

David is actually contrasting between trusting in the strength of chariots and horses and trusting in the name of the Lord. David put his trust in the name of the Lord. He would rely on God alone because God will bring triumph. In those days chariots were quite an impressive weapon of war. They were magnificent. They put on a grand show. The nations put all of their hope in the strength and the number of their war horses. They put all their hope in the strength and the magnificence of their chariots and their vast army of soldiers.

But David considered the name of the God of Jacob far more powerful than trusting in chariots and horses. His testimony was, "We will remember the name of the Lord our God. We will remember our God who we are in covenant with. God has chosen us. We are trusting in our God, the God who chose us." They chose God right there, relying on God who is Jehovah. They were trusting in the name of the God of Jacob who is the independent, indisputable, undeniable, the final, the ever-present God. If David sings this out, then this is also our battle plan. This is our second key—*trust in the name of the God of Jacob*. God never let David down, and He will not let us down.

David wrote many times, "The name of the Lord is a strong tower, the righteous run to it and are safe." He saw this over and over as he went to battle. David was a fighter. He went to war as a fighter. He saw, time and time again, nations trust in the strength of their chariots and horses and armies, and those nations would continually be defeated because David and his army trusted in the name of the Lord.

If we think back to when Saul wanted little bitty David to put on his armor, you know Saul was trusting in the strength of his armor, but David chose to trust in the name of his God. So he chose five smooth stones and he relied upon God. He could have very well seen that God was the only One who would overpower Goliath, and then throughout his life he remembered that God was the only name who could overpower the nations. If we were writing this psalm today, very possibly it would be, "Some trust in nuclear weapons and some trust in their fighter jets, some trust in their army tanks, some trust in their weapons of warfare." It's part of our human nature to actually put our trust in very strong and great things.

But David, in this psalm of military war, shows us to trust in the name of the God of Jacob. We can use this in our own personal life. I think it has amazing personal applications by identifying—what are you trusting in? What chariots and horses in your life are you trusting in possibly more than the Lord?

This is a question to take into your personal prayer time and ask the Holy Spirit to help you identify what you are trusting in. Sometimes it's in our finances. It could be in our job. It could be our house. It could be friends or family. It could be our talent or gifts.

What are the chariots in our life? What are the horses in our life? God wants to be our place of triumph. He wants us to be able to unconditionally say, "I will trust in the name of the Lord." He is the One who delivers.

May the Lord help us to identify that which we trust in more than we trust in His name, because the Lord wants to take us on an amazing adventure of trusting in the name of the God of Jacob. He is our strong defense continually and perpetually.

Sometimes everything is wonderful, but most of the time we are in a battle in which we need God to defend us. We need God to strengthen us and to help us. Psalm 20 will help us not to give up.

What are you going through? Begin to sing this song over your battle. Declare this song over your family. I mean pray this psalm out as a declaration—just like the people did in the day of David. These words will bring confidence and strength and hope in your inner man. These words come alive, and it is literally the Spirit of God strengthening and giving you help. God will give you battle plans. He will give you plans for your battle, and then He will give you victory in your battle.

DAILY PRAYER

Lord, I ask that You show me what gets in the way of complete, 100 percent trust in Your name. Help me to pick up these two simple keys and use them through every battle and all warfare. Oh Lord, reveal every chariot and reveal every horse. I ask for a boost of faith. I ask that You, Lord, enlarge my faith to trust in the name of the Lord.

Oh Lord, I pray this prayer that was prayed over David and this prayer that David answered in confidence to You. May the Lord answer me when I am in distress. In my times of trouble, may He deliver me and answer my cry. May the name of the God of Jacob keep me safe from harm and protect me.

May God give to me every desire and carry out all of my cries, all of my dreams. And Lord, make all my battle plans succeed. Oh Lord, send out Your help. I know that You will send it out. I know the Lord gives victory to His anointed. He answers from His heavenly sanctuary with the victorious power of His right hand. All those who trust Him will rise and stand.

Some trust in chariots, some in horses. Those who trust in their own strength and wisdom—they are brought to their knees and fallen. Oh Lord, some trust in chariots, some in horses, but we trust in the name of the Lord our God, and we rise up and stand firm. Yes, Lord, I stand firm and You answer. God, You answer when I call.

So I stand firm and You answer, God, You answer and give me the victory. God, You delivered Jacob and You rescued David. You are the same all through the ages. You rescue Me today.

Day 20: Write out Psalm 20

- Pray these verses out loud.

- Listen to the soaking for Psalm 3.

- Use these verses to talk to God.

- Can you remember the keys from this psalm?

> *Some trust in chariots, some in horses,*
> *but we trust in the name of the Lord our*
> *God, and we rise up and stand firm.*

NOTES

1. Charles Spurgeon, *The Treasury of David*, "Psalm 20, verse 6," https://archive.spurgeon.org/treasury/treasury.php.
2. Ibid.

Day 21

Anything and Everything

*The king will rejoice in Your strength, O Lord, and in
Your salvation how greatly will he rejoice!*
—Psalm 21:1

*For you have given him his heart's desire,
anything and everything he asks for.*
—Psalm 21:2 TPT

*For the king trusts in the Lord, and by the lovingkindness
of the Most High he will not be moved.*
—Psalm 21:7

Have you ever prayed for something so intensely, you laid out your prayers detail by detail, and then, one by one, everything you prayed *happened* and every request was answered in the way that you were asking these prayers to be answered? Can you remember a time when you could not be more specific? Every tiny cry, every request down to the tiniest plea—God answered and worked everything out in the exact way you had prayed for it to work out?

Well, this is the feeling that David had as he was coming home from the battle. In fact, his testimony was, "Anything and everything

I asked from You, God, You gave to me." In Psalm 20, we find David riding out to fight the battle, and in Psalm 21, David is coming home singing his victory song. He's victorious and he is telling the stories of the wonders of God in the midst of the battle. He is telling of the glories and the power of the hand of God that delivered David and all his men in the battle. We are putting ourselves in the storyline of Psalm 21. It's our cry. Psalm 21 is our celebration song of thanksgiving to God. It flows together perfectly with Psalm 20, declaring, "The victory belongs to the Lord." Only God gives victories. David gives credit to no other man, nor to his army, nor to the strength of horses or chariots. As Kidner writes, "Only God and David are in the picture in these verses."[1] And David credits all of this to the strength of the Lord.

David shows us some keys that I believe helped him win the battle. Here lies our first key in Psalm 21—*Your strength, or the Lord's strength*. In Psalm 21, we find David singing, "I will rejoice in *Your strength*." In Psalm 20, David determined to set his eyes upon the Lord and trust in the name of the God of Jacob even before the battle was fought. Here he comes home singing and declaring his great victory and gives all credit to the strength of the Lord. His testimony, his song, his declaration was *Your strength*—the strength of the Lord who in the battle made David strong. This is a powerful and crucial key to use in our lives. That strength that David found in the midst of his battle was all wrapped up in the leaning.

This was his confession as he went out to battle and it was his song of praise when he came home victorious. He boldly proclaimed that the Lord, whom he trusted in as he went out to battle, was the complete reason he won the battle. David gives all credit to the Lord and to His strength. This key, *Your strength,* can mean force, security, majesty, might, boldness, power (Strong's H5797). What does that look like to lean on the force of God? To trust and have confidence in the security of God as arrows are aimed right in your direction with the intent to kill. How does one truly feel secure in the midst of the fight? Well, David tells us right at the beginning of this psalm. Maybe he pulled out those keys and sang loud, "I find all my joy in the might of God. I find all my peace in the power of God who fought with me and for me in this battle."

This is a powerful key—*Your strength.* As David leaned on and trusted in the strength of the Lord, he became strong. When he leaned on the boldness and power of God, that same boldness and power arose within David all throughout the battle. This same key will work for us in every battle or crisis we find ourselves in. Just like the Lord's strength steadied David, His strength will steady us.

David continues his song of praise and thanksgiving with key number two—*anything and everything.* David's testimony was, "God, You gave me anything and everything that I asked for." Other translations say, "You have given him his heart's desire" (TPT). In the battle, You gave him everything he asked for in prayer. This key, *anything and everything,* is an invitation for us to ask for everything. Ask God for every victory. Ask God for as much as you can possibly think of asking to set yourself up for a big win in every battle that you face. "Now all glory to God, who is able, through his mighty power at work within us, to accomplish infinitely more than we might ask or think" (Eph. 3:20 NLT).

This key, *anything and everything,* assures us that what God gave to David, He will do the same for us. God gave to David his heart's desire. That word *desire* can mean "longing, exceedingly." It paints a word picture here of being totally greedy (Strong's H5797). "I want it all and God told me I could have it." You will not want to leave this key behind or forget it at home; you will want to use this upon every prayer and request to God—*anything and everything*.

Right here, David begins to sing out of the overflow in his heart as verse after verse he decrees who God is and what God has done for him. Then he gladly responds to his own song with a prophetic decree over his life. This might very well have been the chorus to such a triumphant song. There is a response right here that literally erupts within David like a volcano that is exploding. Unable to keep these words inside any longer, he makes this decree about himself— *because I trust in the Lord, and by the loving kindness of God, I will not be moved.*

It is almost as if David grabs these two keys—*Your strength* and *anything and everything*—then sings out, "I will not be moved. I'm going to keep wholeheartedly leaning upon the Lord's strength, and I'm going to continue to ask for *anything and everything.*" David trusts in God all the more. And the theme of the song begins to shift right here. The foundations of the song are these two keys as David sings loud of the loving kindness of the Most High, "God, You are so good to me. God, You are so kind to me," and then David's declaration is, "I will never be moved. Battles won't shake me. People will not cause me to stumble. My foundation remains strong because my eyes are upon the Most High. Spurgeon writes, "Other kings fail because they rest upon an arm of flesh, but our monarch reigns on in splendour because he trusteth in Jehovah."[1]

We can say the same thing that David said over his life: "My God also gives me anything and everything I ask for. He helps me in all my battles. He heals my body. He answers every request perfectly, and because of Him my foundation is strong, my heart is steady, I will not be shaken, and I will not be moved. My trust in God shifts into a whole new place, and my proclamation is my triumphant theme. This is personal because this is who I have become. I will not be shaken. I will never be moved because of the loving kindness of the Lord."

Oh, let's pick up these keys and use them. They will cause us to have expectant faith that arises in the midst of our battles. They will help us to expect a victory even before the battle is over.

This song of David is also our song. This is our promise. This is our right as a believer. It's our guarantee. We are His favorite ones, and when people look at our life, may they be able to see in us and say about us, "Wow, they are overflowing in blessing even in the midst of their battle. They are so steady." Using these two keys will cause a heart response just like David had.

For the king trusts in the Lord, and by the loving-kindness of the Most High he will not be moved.

DAILY PRAYER

Oh Lord, You make me joyful by Your presence. I put my trust in You forever. I will not be moved. Your love never fails me. Your love surrounds me. I rejoice in Your strength with shouts of joy because You have given me the victory and I'm bursting out with a joyful song, oh God. You have given me my heart's desire. Anything and everything I asked for You did for me, not withholding anything.

You surrounded me with protection; You gave me inner strength. You surround me with Your unfailing love. What else could I ask for? What else do I need? You surrounded me; You did not withhold from Your beloved one. I am Your beloved one.

God, You make me joyful in Your presence, and I put my trust in You forever, *and rich blessings overflow with every encounter I have with You.*

I asked You to save me and You said yes. I am Your beloved one and You are my pure and shining radiating One. Rise up! Put Your might on display. We will sing and praise Your glorious power. We will sing and celebrate Your mighty act.

Day 21: Write out Psalm 21

- Pray these verses out loud.
- Listen to the soaking for Psalm 21.
- Can you put yourself in the storyline of Psalm 21?
- Can you remember the keys from this psalm?

> *You surround me with Your unfailing love. What else could I ask for?*

NOTES

1. Charles Spurgeon, *The Treasury of David*, "Psalm 21, verse 7," https://archive.spurgeon.org/treasury/treasury.php.

Week 4

Day 22

A Portrait of the Cross

My God, my God, why have You forsaken me? Why are You so far
from delivering me, and from my roaring words of distress?
O my God, I cry in the daytime, but You do not answer;
and at night, but I have no rest. But You are holy,
—Psalm 22:1-3

Has there ever been such a paradox between title and prose? Even the title itself is an oxymoron showing the vast gulf between beauty and anguish. The portrait is a painting, a picture full of life, a pictorial representation of a person usually showing the face. Psalm 22 shows the contrast of beauty and abandonment, of complete trust yet groaning anguish, of sorrow yet joy, of death yet life. David starts with his groaning and walks us through his wrestling as his deep emotions make the loudest of sounds and his feelings of abandonment seem nearer than God's presence.

This psalm originally gave voice to the plight of the pious, the God-fearing, or the devoted, despite the advance of the wicked. It is not so different from the topic of Job, Lamentations, Proverbs, and other psalms. It is a song of submission despite distance, one of acceptance in the face of rejection. It is a dichotomy between what one hopes and what one lives.[1]

It is similar to Psalm 10 when David writes, "Lord You seem so far away, and darkness seems so near. Why do You hide Yourself, just when I need You most?" Have you ever heard yourself cry out with the deepest and most intense groan that comes out of the depths of your body? It is a loud sound—*God, where are You?* This is the cry that David had in Psalm 22. *The Passion Translation* says:

> *God, my God! Why would you abandon me now? Why do you remain distant, refusing to answer my tearful cries in the day and my desperate cries for your help in the night? I can't stop sobbing. Where are you, my God? Yet I know that you are most holy; it's indisputable. You are God-Enthroned, surrounded with songs, living among the shouts of praise of your princely people* (Psalm 22:1-3 TPT).

There is no reference to sin as the cause of the trouble, no plea of innocence, no claim of righteousness, and no vengeance. Therefore, the words are peculiarly appropriate of the suffering Messiah, although in the primary meaning they are based on some experience of the psalmist.[2]

David cries out, "My God, my God." From the depths of his groan he is crying, "You are my God. My almighty God, my great God. My God of all power. My God of all might. My God, the strong One, who is good." All of these words were wrapped up into one cry, "My God," and this cry was repeated again, "My God." These words were written two times to show emphasis and great need in this cry (Strong's H410).

He cries, "My God." This is our first key for Psalm 22—*my God, my God*. He is mine. David cries, "You are *my* God. You are not only the God of my father or the God of Jacob. You are my God." This must be our cry also. My God, You are mine. David brings us on a real journey and lets us peer into his cry where he feels utterly abandoned and alone. In this aloneness, the presence of God, which he is so used to being surrounded by, seems gone—so David reminds himself in this cry, *My God, and I say it again, my God.*

This is a critical key we must carry all throughout life. In the seasons of crisis and hopelessness, in seasons of desperation and chaos, we must simply pull out this key and cry out this cry. *My God, my God.* You are the One I cry out to. You are the first One I lift my voice to. You are my God, and I remind myself even again with this key—*my God, my God.* He is mine and I am His, forever and ever.

David continues his cry with very real questions in need of very real answers: "Why have You forsaken me? God, where are You? I cannot feel You anywhere. Why did You leave me? Why have You left me alone? I feel deserted by the One I need the most" (Strong's H5800).

These are real cries that we can use and embrace in seasons of desperation when we feel alone. David goes on to cry out, "You are far away. You feel so far in the distance. I cannot even see You, though I look for You with every breath. It feels like there is a great distance between You and me. The time goes on and on as I am in great need of deliverance. *My God, my God,* I need You close. I need You to bring forth a victory in my life. I want to feel safe in the nearness of Your presence, yet I feel the gulf between us."

Here again, we find a very real psalm that will give us language to have an ongoing conversation with God all throughout the crisis, or all throughout the grief and heartbreak when there seem to be no answers. Seasons and times of great grief can be where we get off track as we have no words. This psalm will give us language and keep us continually talking to the One we need the most as we groan from heartbreak and don't have the words to speak. Psalm 22 is our words. It keeps the lines of continual communion with God ongoing.

Then David uses the word *roar* to describe the *sound* of his deep groan of anguish. Do you know this sound? Have you ever heard the sound of this cry coming from the depths of your being? Psalm 22 gives us permission to cry out when we have no understanding. It gives us permission to make the sounds of a groan only known to the most broken of hearts and to the one feeling great distance from the only One who can save. This word *roar* is the sound like a lion's roar. It is a cry or moan of distress. *Strong's Concordance* tells us this cry is like the sound of a wretched person wrung forth by grief (Strong's H7581). It is the sound of a brokenhearted person; it is the sound of someone grief-stricken. This is the sound that the human soul understands, yet is unable to console—this is that roar.

It is the sound of Rachel: "A voice is heard in Ramah, lamentation and bitter weeping, Rachel weeping for her children, refusing to be comforted for her children, because they are no more" (Jer. 31:15). This was fulfilled in Matthew 2:18. In Job 3:24: "For my sighing comes before I eat, and my groaning pours forth like the waters." This is a real sound of the deepest of grief, the deepest of distress. David writes, "I cry in the daytime and I cry in the nighttime." This is not a one-time roar or groan; it is an agonizing sound that is not always solved in a day. It may take a season. It may take longer. The length of the groan is not the focus, but the continual cry of the words of David. As long as it takes, as long as you need to groan from the deepest places, keep this key, *my God, my God*, close. And use the words of David all along the way to keep open communion with God, who is the only one who can heal in the deepest places of our soul and being.

In the midst of the cry, here we find our second key from Psalm 22. This place right here is our landing place. *You are holy*. This is our second key—*You are holy*. No matter what we face, no matter the turbulent storms and torrents of rushing waters that we walk through, *You are holy*. This is why we can trust You, God. This is our key, no matter what comes our way. We always land here—*You are holy*. David says out loud, "I don't have an answer yet, I still feel inside the grief of distance, yet I will pull out this key—*You are holy*. I will remind myself all through the sorrow that *this* is who You are. *You are holy*. You are set apart. You are like no one or nothing else. You are God. You are divine."

We can pull out these two keys. We can walk through the details of the emotional wrestle of David, *my God, my God,* and yet make our landing place be, *You are holy*. This is the beginning. This is the end. And this is the whole middle of the storyline—*You are holy*.

David makes it totally clear. He writes it out with his pen—*You are holy*. In the midst of my trials, in the midst of my suffering, in the midst of my crisis, in the midst of my pain and the anguish that I felt in my body—*You are holy*. David does not write from the place of cursing and blaspheming God. He settles it with his pen in his hand and writes, "But I know You are holy." Even though he knew the agony of his present pain, he wrote, "You are good even in this great suffering." This is David's truth. This is his reality—*God is holy*.

Then, maybe every step of David's life, maybe every key he would ever use or choice that he would ever make—maybe that led up to this moment. Right here, it is as if he steps into a future time. David with his pen in hand begins to write about a greater David who would, word for word, go through and cry out every detail written from Psalm 22. David has a full encounter of Jesus, the Son of David, on the cross, writing detail by detail words that David said in his day that Jesus would cry out generations later. He writes of actual events that would take place. It is almost as if David steps into the future, seeing Jesus on the cross as he writes the actual details of the crucifixion. David perfectly describes Psalm 22, which is the portrait of the cross. To the pure and shining one. His life poured out for us. Yes, He gave it all for love.

The cross—a symbol of life eternal yet also the symbol of suffering. People wear crosses every day as a symbol of beauty. Some wear the cross as jewelry without even knowing the meaning behind such a symbol. Others wear crosses as a remembrance of the suffering and beating that Jesus endured for the sake of every sinner, once and for all, bridging the gap between God and man.

In this psalm David sings much more than as an artist; he also sings as one of the greatest prophets to speak. David's own experience is obviously reflected in this psalm but even in a greater matter—it points to the experience of Jesus Christ, the son of David, David's greater son. Spurgeon writes:

This is beyond all others the Psalm of the Cross. It may have been actually repeated word by word by our Lord when hanging on the tree; it would be too bold to say that it was so, but even a casual reader may see that it might have been. ...It is the photograph of our Lord's saddest hours, the record of his dying words, the lachrymatory of his last tears, the memorial of his expiring joys.[3]

Jesus in His body was the only man who experienced the wrath of God. Jesus took our place. He was a substitute for all of humanity. He was a substitute for you and for me in active love. Jesus Christ fulfilled God's good and loving plan of redemption. He bore the separation, the abandonment, and the wrath of God in that one act of love—dying on the cross.

Even though David felt abandoned, he was not entirely abandoned. He felt separated from God, though he never was. In Psalm 22, David brings us with him into the future as he sees Jesus, feeling once and for all the abandonment and the wrath of God. David saw into the future as Jesus, in His body, felt and endured the wrath of God out of His perfect love for man. Jesus endured anguish, He was beaten beyond the form of a man, and He personally experienced abandonment and separation that even David did not experience, and we will *never* experience this abandonment from God.

David Guzik said, "We feel a bit like we're on holy ground. ... It so powerfully and so beautifully and so movingly describes in prophecy the sufferings of Jesus who specifically referred to this psalm [Psalm 22], even on the Cross."[4] Here is our third key—*we are not abandoned.* Jesus took that abandonment once and for all upon Himself.

DAILY PRAYER

My God, my God, why have You forsaken me, abandoned me, why are You far from the words of my groaning? It's a portrait of the cross of the pure and shining One. His life poured out for us when He gave it all for love. God, what a beautiful portrait.

Lord, You made me trust in You, and You have been my God. Do not be far from me. For trouble is near and there is no one to help.

Evil men have encircled me, they have pierced my hands and my feet, they divide my garments among them and cast lots for my clothing. Oh my strength, come quickly to help me. Deliver me and rescue me. I will declare Your name. I will praise You.

You have become the theme of my praise. I will fulfill my vows and the poor will eat and be satisfied. They who seek the Lord will praise Him. I will sing praise. For the Lord is King over all the earth, and the whole world will remember the Lord and turn to Him and bow down low and praise Him.

Those not yet born will serve the Lord and hear from us the wonders of our God. A future generation, they will glorify and testify and hear from us the wonders of our God.

Day 22: Write out Psalm 22

- Pray these verses out loud.
- Listen to the soaking for Psalm 22.
- Can you put yourself in the storyline of Psalm 22?
- Can you remember the keys from this psalm?

> *The portrait of the cross to the pure and shining One. His life poured out for us when He gave it all for love.*

NOTES

1. Joseph Meyer, formerly a Doctoral Fellow in Classical Languages and Literature at UCSB.

2. Pfeiffer and Harrison, *The Wycliffe Bible Commentary*, 503.

3. Charles Spurgeon, *The Treasury of David*, "Psalm 22, Subject," https://archive.spurgeon.org/treasury/treasury.php.

4. David Guzzik, "Psalm 22: The Servant of God Forsaken, Rescued, and Triumphant," YouTube, July 11, 2020, https://www.youtube.com/watch?v=5wHOF0_pyQo.

Day 23

Complete Reliance

The Lord is my shepherd; I shall not want.
—Psalm 23:1

Sitting on the front pew in church one Sunday morning, I heard the pastor read, "*The Lord is my Shepherd; I shall not want.*" I still have a memory of looking down at my shiny black patent leather shoes with the big silver buckle, white short bobby socks with lace, and my skinned knees, thinking, "What is a shepherd?" As the pastor began to unwrap what I am sure were amazing nuggets from Psalm 23, I was stuck on those words: "The Lord is my Shepherd; I shall not want."

Our family lived in Belvue, Kansas, population 170, until I was eight years old. I attended the Belvue United Methodist Church built alongside a gravel road right off Highway 24. It was a lovely little church with a white steeple and a bell that would ring at the start of Sunday service. My mom would drop me off for Sunday school, and on a rare occasion I would stay for the weekly church service and sing in the choir.

Now this verse was quite perplexing to me as a six-year-old girl. Instead of two complete statements: "The Lord is my Shepherd. I shall not want," I lumped them all together as, "The Lord is a Shepherd, and I don't want Him." A little girl from Kansas might not understand the true meaning of a Shepherd but many years later, I understood clearly who He was and how much I needed Him and wanted Him.

We find shepherds all throughout the Word. Being a shepherd was not a glamorous job. In fact, it was the lowest job one could have on the social scale. Shepherds lived in the fields with their sheep. Yet many patriarchs of old were shepherds; among them were Abraham and Jacob, Moses, King David, and Amos. In the Gospel of John, Jesus calls Himself the Good Shepherd who lays down His life for the sheep. In fact, in the Middle Eastern culture, shepherds are most often the young girls of the family, unless there are no daughters. That throws a whole new twist into the storyline of David and his brothers.

What does the shepherd do?

The shepherd watches over and provides for the sheep. He meets their every need. He protects them around every turn and every deep ravine. He provides everything. This is a psalm of complete dependence and total reliance on the Lord. For we are His sheep, and our sole provider and protector is the Lord. There is no one else or nothing else that will provide and care for the sheep.

In the year 2020, the crisis of a worldwide pandemic hit every nation and every people group. Suddenly people could not lean on their jobs or skills. The whole world came to a standstill one weekend in March 2020, with governmental mandatory quarantines, businesses closing, churches closing. Thanksgiving was canceled in many places, and even Christmas was canceled as far as families gathering together. The year 2020 brought many people to the very end of their means. Every crutch that seemed to help people walk through life was yanked away.

The whole believing world found themselves as sheep needing a Shepherd. Life as everyone had known it suddenly stopped as everyone began asking, "God, what do we do? Help me. Lead me. Feed me, God."

The true meaning of this verse became the highlight of every day throughout 2020—the Lord is my Shepherd. Suddenly, this psalm of complete reliance upon God came to light in every place. We *are* the sheep. We are looking for a leader, for a shepherd whom we can trust to lead us, protect us, and provide for us, much like in the days when David actually wrote this psalm.

David most likely wrote this psalm in the desert. I heard in a teaching from Ray Vander Laan that the desert is a place where only God provides. God provided water out of a rock, manna from the sky, a pillar of fire that lead by night, and a cloud that lead by day. It's a tabernacle where the Israelites met God intimately. The desert is a place where they learned to trust God completely. In the desert, God's people learned to love Him, trust Him, and have all their confidence in Him.

We have read all of the Scriptures and sung the songs, memorized every place where a shepherd is highlighted in the Word. Now we are invited to live like David did in complete trust and confidence in *the Lord, who is our Shepherd*. Here lies our first key in Psalm 23—*the Lord is my Shepherd*. This is our key for life. The Lord, Jah, the Creator, our God, the Self-Existent One, our life sustainer—He is our Shepherd. He is personal. He is my Shepherd.

This is a must for us as we navigate the waters of plagues, financial loss, and crises. *The Lord is my Shepherd*—we have talked about this in other psalms. He is not just the God of my father, but He is my God, my shepherd. Hold this key close. In fact, make some copies of this key and wear it as a necklace. Hang it anywhere and everywhere you look to remind yourself there is One greater whose promise it is to provide, protect, comfort, and lead.

David Kidner writes, "The shepherd lives with his flock and is everything to it: guide, physician and protector."[1] As David was writing this psalm, he had an understanding that sheep are 100 percent reliant upon the shepherd for their every need—so he related his life with the Lord in the very same way. The sheep have a complete understanding of the sound of their shepherd's voice, and they will never follow another voice; they will only follow the voice they know.

When we unwrap the word *Shepherd,* He is my teacher, He feeds me, He takes me to a place where I can eat, He is my companion who provides for me. He provides just the right amount of food at the right time—and then every sheep looks to the shepherd to provide the next bite.

Now when we bring in the Greek, it's "The Lord shepherds me or the Lord herds me, and nothing will be lacking (from) me." The two elements of interest to me are that the writer emphasizes the activity a shepherd performs instead of labeling God as a shepherd—there is an active, progressive, and present force that God continues to herd the godly person. Moreover, the second idea is in the future—there is a relationship between the *present* shepherding of God and the *future* lack of nothing.[2]

So where are the green pastures?

I have been to Israel; I did not see one green pasture, nor did I see any knee-high fields with green grass for sheep to graze upon. In reading Psalm 23, my mind always saw plenty of green pastures, with beautiful lakes and still waters, but in reality when I went to Israel I did not see any. The desert was pretty barren, with no green pastures and no lush river banks with flowing, fresh water. If you ever go to Israel and are able to follow the footsteps of the young shepherds, you will see rocks, sand, stones, more rocks, pebbles, and lots of dirt. It is hot in the day with very little shade, and it is cold at night.

In the desert, there is not an abundance of grazing; there is just enough for what each sheep needs at the time. When it comes time for the next meal, each sheep is totally reliant upon the shepherd to find the next nibble or the next bite. From a distance, it looks like the sheep are grazing on stones and rocks, but they are actually eating tiny blades of grass.

What happens in Israel is that at night, warm, moist air from the Mediterranean blows across the desert. When that humid air hits the side of a dry hill, it condenses and waters the ground just enough for a tuft of baby grass to pop up overnight. This grass is just enough for the sheep to get one mouthful, and then they have to look toward the shepherd to say, "Where is the next mouthful?"[3] In the same way, we have to trust our Great Shepherd to lead us every step of the way. We are not walking in green fields of knee-deep grass. We must have total reliance upon our Shepherd.

When we use this key, *the Lord is my Shepherd*, if our complete reliance is upon the Lord through famine, through plagues, through sickness, through every crisis the world would throw at us, the rest of the psalm will begin to unwrap. It leads us on a journey of leaning upon Him all of the days of our life as we trust His perfect leadership. If we cannot walk out the first five words, *the Lord is my Shepherd*, if we miss this key, then we will miss the whole psalm. This is an invitation of complete and utter reliance. Not just for a day but for complete trust and dependence upon the Shepherd to lead throughout our entire life.

In a world where people strive to show their own strength and want to make their own path, Psalm 23 shows us the wisdom of following and relying upon the Lord. It shows us that the Lord is our sole provider and protector. This is wisdom. This is strength. Pull out this key, *the Lord is my Shepherd*, hold it close, look at these words often, say them out loud, and follow.

The next key is *I shall not want*, meaning "I have everything I need and I will trust the Shepherd for more when I need more." David experienced both sides of this reality. He started his journey as a young shepherd, then suddenly found himself the leader and provider of people.

Psalm 23 has stood by the Jewish people as their support through the darkest days of persecution and exile. Over the centuries, no evil murderer or terrible tragedy has been able to crush the resilient spirit of the Jews, when they remember that "You are with me" (verse 4).[4]

So pick up these two keys and hold them close. When the old north winds begin to blow, pull out these two keys *the Lord is my Shepherd* and *I shall not want*. I will take out my first key, *the Lord is my Shepherd*, and as I walk in the reality of this I am able to confidently say, "I have everything I need." Lord, I have all I need in You.

DAILY PRAYER

The Lord is my Shepherd; I shall not want. The Lord is my Shepherd; I have everything. I have all I need in You. You make me lie down in green pastures. You lead me beside the quiet waters. Lord, You restore my soul and guide me in the path of righteousness, all for Your name's sake.

Though walking through the valley of the shadow of death, fear will never conquer me, for You already have. You remain close to me, and through it all You lead. Your authority, it is my strength and it is my peace. You prepare a table right before me in the presence of all my enemies. You, my Shepherd, have prepared my delicious feast. When my enemies dare to fight against me, You anoint my head with oil and my cup overflows. Surely goodness and Your unfailing love, oh, they will chase me down all of my days. And I will dwell in the house of the Lord forever and forevermore.

Day 23: Write out Psalm 23

- Pray these verses out loud.

- Listen to the soaking for Psalm 23.

- Can you put yourself in the storyline of Psalm 23?

- Can you remember the keys from this psalm?

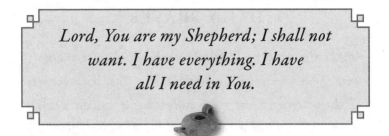

Lord, You are my Shepherd; I shall not want. I have everything. I have all I need in You.

NOTES

1. Kidner, *Psalms*, 127.

2. Joseph Meyer, formerly a Doctoral Fellow in Classical Languages and Literature at UCSB.

3. In addition to my own experiences, Ray Vander Laan discusses this same phenomenon and describes what Bedouin shepherds taught him in "The Lord Is My Shepherd," YouTube, https://www.youtube.com/watch?v=JfPOqM3N9kg.

4. The Israel Bible Online, "Psalm 23," 23:6, https://theisraelbible.com/bible/psalms/chapter-23.

Day 24

Armed and Ready
for Battle

*The earth is the Lord's, and everything in it. The world and all its
people belong to him. ...Who is the King of glory? The Lord,
strong and mighty; the Lord, invincible in battle.*
—Psalm 24:1,8,10 NLT

In 1974, as a brand-new freshman at Wamego High School, under the leadership of John Childs, our high school marching band was chosen to play in the New York City Macy's Day Parade. Our marching band began to get ready for this event, showing up ninety minutes before school ever started, we practiced marching in straight lines all throughout the streets of Wamego Kansas, memorizing all the songs. We had marching steps to each song, dance moves, songs to memorize, and important turns. We practiced marching and lifting our knees high so that the marching line looked flawless. The day finally came when we were off to New York City. It was my first time out of Kansas, my first time on an airplane, my first time in a big city, my first time seeing skyscrapers. On Thanksgiving morning, we had a 3:30 A.M. alarm set to get dressed and get down to find our place in the parade. We walked

32 blocks in the freezing cold following a dozen horses. This was the biggest crowd of people cheering I had ever seen. They were lined for miles to watch every part of this joyous event. Oh, what a parade. The music, the shouting, the joy, the drum cadence, the floats, all of the marching bands. The triumphant sounds echoing all throughout the streets of New York City and to top off the whole parade was Santa Claus. Everywhere I looked, throngs of people were cheering and full of joy as each band and each float made its way down the streets of New York City.

In Psalm 24, we find David hosting the parade of all parades. The whole kingdom had come out to witness the return of the Ark of the Covenant to the City of David. This parade lined from the house of Obed-Edom to the hill of Mount Zion.

> *David danced before the Lord with all his might, wearing a priestly garment. So David and all the people of Israel brought up the Ark of the Lord with shouts of joy and the blowing of rams' horns* (2 Samuel 6:14-15 NLT).

All of Israel celebrated the Ark of the Covenant, welcomed to the hill of Zion. There was only one who did not enjoy this parade, to which David responded, "I can be even more undignified than this." The day of *this* parade full of joyful shouts, singing, dancing, declarations, and music was the setting for Psalm 24.

So picture in your mind David with his grand parade of musicians, singers, choruses, and musical instruments. The Levites carrying the Ark of The Covenant. All the people singing and shouting, "The earth is the Lord's and everything and everyone in it is His."

Spurgeon writes, "The whole round world is claimed for Jehovah, 'and they that dwell therein' are declared to be his subjects."[1]

Here lies our first key: "*The earth is the Lord's.*" This declaration that started David's song needs to be the declaration that starts ours. The entire world belongs to God. Everything is God's. Everyone belongs to God. This settles any and all questions because it is all from God, created by God and for God. When we unwrap some of these words, the *earth* means "countries, territories, districts, regions, tribal territories, all inhabitants of the land, Sheol, land without return, city, states, ground, soil." Then it is every people, every land, every country—we could go on and on—but it is every single thing belongs to the Lord. Now when we bring in the Greek for this verse, the Greek is, "The earth (is) the Lord's and its sum." What's interesting is that the emphasis in Greek is on the Lord due to word order. Thus, even though the idea of the sentence is "everything belongs to the Lord," God still remains the focal point amidst everything else that He owns.[2]

This is our statement. This is our key. This is the truth: "The earth is the Lord's and everything in it belongs to Him."

This psalm is very similar to Psalm 15, which many believe was sung when David began to bring the Ark of the Covenant up the first time which brought about the death of Uzzah as the oxen stumbled and he reached out to steady the Ark of the Covenant. Therefore, David writes in the middle section the rules for carrying the presence of the Lord. Now we will not be carrying The Ark of the Covenant, however, we do carry the presence of the Lord within us. So think of the Holy Spirit alive within us just as the presence of God was alive in the Ark. Therefore, the middle portion are steps and directions we need to follow.

There is an obedience that we are invited to walk in as we carry the presence of the Lord on a continual basis. So when we pick up this first key, *the earth is the Lord's, it* sends us down the right path much like Psalm 1 does when we follow those directions. Then Psalm 24 asks the very same questions that Psalm 15 asked. Who may ascend the hill of the Lord? Who may stand in His presence? Two different times in the Psalms, David is asking this question and then giving us the instructions. This is our heads up. It has to do with our hands, our heart, and our mouth. Carrying or hosting the presence of the Lord is a privilege—it is an honor that requires our hands, our heart, and our mouth. This to me speaks again as in previous psalms that the eyes of the Lord are always watching our private lives. What we do in private matters. He wants to empower us to live rightly before Him when no one is looking. When it's just you and the Lord, He wants to help every believer make right choices. He wants to bring everything into the light. And He requires this as He promises to help us achieve right choices at all times so that the presence of God we carry in our lives in public is the overflow of our life in God before the eyes of One—before the Lord alone.

We have our key, *the earth is the Lord's*, which leads us straight to the question: Who can host the presence of the Lord continually? This leads us to God's view of our private lives and His desire to strengthen us for righteous choices involving our hands, our heart, and our mouth. I like to call this the "heads up passage" because this passageway leads us straight into the joyful celebration of David's parade in the last four verses.

Many believe these last couple of verses were literally a song. As David begins to declare, "Open up the gates," this was antiphonally sung, meaning David would sing out parts of it and then the people would respond in singing back to David. It would have been a grand chorus that they continued to remember, much like the "Hallelujah" chorus by George Frideric Handel. They would have practiced this song so that everyone knew their part as the Ark of the Covenant made its way up to Jerusalem

They would have sung out, "Lift up your heads, O gates, and be lifted up, you everlasting doors, that the King of Glory may come in." Then there was a chorus of voices from within the gates of Jerusalem actually welcoming the Ark of the Covenant in. They would have sung, "Who is this King of Glory? The Lord strong and mighty. The Lord mighty in battle." Then picture a chorus of priests, Levites and people outside the gates with the Ark, and they are answering them in verse 9, saying, "Lift up your heads, O gates, and lift them up you everlasting doors that the King of Glory may come in." Then the voices within the gates begin to declare and sing out, "Who is this King of Glory? The Lord of hosts; He is the King of Glory." Then the whole grand chorus of everyone would have sung that last verse, "Who is this King of Glory? It's Adonai—He is the King of Glory." Then Selah—pause and think about that.

They are singing, "Open up the gates" as they watch the literal gates of Jerusalem be lifted up to welcome back the Ark of the Covenant.

In the same way that the Ark of the Covenant went through the gates—as the crowds were singing, children were rejoicing, and the musicians were playing—David begins to see into the future, into the day when Jesus Christ, the King of Glory, the Lord strong and mighty will be welcomed back to Jerusalem with the gates of the city lifted up and the parade of all parades welcoming *Yeshua Hamashiach* back into Jerusalem.

Here lies another key for us—*who is this King of Glory?* This is a real question that we want to ask ourselves. Who is this King? He is the King of all nations and He is the King of our hearts. This King fights on our behalf today. He is the victorious One. He is armed and ready for battle. He is victorious over everything. He is mighty over sin, mighty over hell, and mighty over death. This mighty King fights on our behalf today. Whatever we face. Whatever our battle. This King is armed and ready to fight with us and for us. We are not alone. We are never left without help. We have this promise of Psalm 24. This is our key—*we have a King who fights for us and with us.* He is mighty. He is glorious, and He cares about our battles.

So what battle are you fighting? What are you fighting in your life where you feel the enemy coming against you? I want you to picture the King of Glory, the King of Heaven's armies, this great warrior. He is armed, and He is ready to fight with you and for you in battle. You do not fight alone. You have the King of the host of Heaven's armies, and He is armed and ready to help you fight your battle.

Remember this King—He's victorious over everything; nothing hinders Him. Nothing stops Him. The King of Glory is behind you, beside you, in front of you. We are surrounded by His shield, by His presence, and He is victorious over everything. He's the One who is helping us fight our battle. So let this be a twofold song. Let it call us higher in how we live our lives, the choices that we make when no one's looking, the words that we use in life when no one is around to hear. God hears. How we live our lives when no one's looking, this is what the King of Glory is in battle over—that we are upright and righteous when no one is looking. Oh, that we would be those who ascend, who come up and commune with the Holy Spirit and commune with God and host His mighty presence wherever we go.

DAILY PRAYER

Oh Lord, The earth is the Lord's, and everything in it belongs to You. The whole world is Yours, and everyone in it belongs to You. You founded it upon the sea, established it upon the waters; You are the One who pushed back the ocean to let the dry land appear.

Lord, who may ascend the hill of the Lord, and who may stand in His holy place? Who may ascend to the presence of the Lord? God, could it me? Let me be one who has clean hands and a pure heart, whose works and ways are pure, and whose heart is true. Oh, let me be the one who never deceives, whose words are sure.

I seek You, God of Jacob, I want to stand before You, seeking the pleasure of Your face, seeking out the pleasure of Your ways.

So be lifted up, O you gates. Be lifted up you ancient doors; let the King of Glory come in. Who is this King of Glory? He is the Lord, strong and mighty. He is the Lord, mighty in battle. He conquers everything.

Day 24: Write out Psalm 24

- Pray these verses out loud.

- Listen to the soaking for Psalm 24.

- Can you put yourself in the storyline of Psalm 24?

- Can you remember the keys from this psalm?

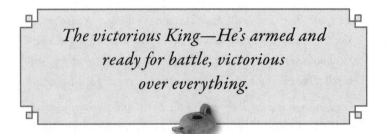

The victorious King—He's armed and ready for battle, victorious over everything.

NOTES

1. Spurgeon, *The Treasury of David*, "Psalm 24, verse 1."

2. Joseph Meyer, formerly a Doctoral Fellow in Classical Languages and Literature at UCSB.

Our Reserved Seat

Show me the right path, O Lord; point out the road for me to follow.
Lead me by your truth and teach me, for you are the God
who saves me. All day long I put my hope in you.
—Psalm 25:4-5 NLT

There's a private place reserved for the lovers of God, where they sit
near him and receive the revelation-secrets of his promises.
—Psalm 25:14 TPT

Have you ever been invited to a special event where you were told, "We have a reserved seat for you"? I love reserved seats. You get to sit up close. You can see well, and you can hear well. You don't have to get there super early to stand in line just to get a good seat, because you have a reserved seat. In reserved seating, one has to be invited to be able to sit in that section. There was one meeting I still remember when I found my name on a reserved seat. As I began to sit down, I heard some-one fast approaching me and yelling, "Did you take my seat? That was my seat!" #YIKES. I promise, I didn't take anyone's seat. I have actually been to many different meetings, dinners, or conferences that I have found myself in the front, in the back, in the middle, and I have to say being invited to the reserved seating area is always a plus. In Psalm 25, we find David writing about this reserved seating area, and he lets us know who this seating area is for and what is spoken in these reserved seats.

Most commentaries agree that David wrote this psalm in his later days. As David is remembering his many failures, he is also remembering God's great mercy over his life. He is remembering his many times of distress, but is reminded of God's faithfulness throughout each season.

But David asks a question in Psalm 25:4 that I have personally asked many times throughout my life. In fact, I have heard many people ask this same question: "Show me the right path, O Lord, point out the road for me to follow." At this time in David's life he cries out, "Lord, You show me Your path. It is the right path, and that is the only path I want to find myself walking down."

Here lies our first key—*show me the right path*. Lord, You show me. I will follow wherever You show me I need to be.

This is an important key because it keeps our eyes focused on the Lord and His will and perfect plan for our lives. Should we want to go our own way, this key will bring us back to the place we need to be, looking at the Lord and asking Him again, "Show us the way." I do not believe that the Lord gets tired of hearing this request, nor does He get tired of answering it. I think He loves to hear these keys jingling in our pockets.

The word *show* can mean "to be instructed, to become aware by seeing." It can mean "to acquire knowledge, to see and then know, to see and observe with the eyes." It can mean "to discover by seeing or hearing" (Strong's H3045). This key will continually keep us leaning on the Lord, looking to Him who knows the absolute best way for our lives, and it is a promise that when we ask God to show us, He will show us the way. He will instruct us and help us. David says, "As I go on this journey all throughout my life, God will point out the road for me to follow. Then we simply walk down that path in complete trust because God showed us; He pointed us down the right path. And it is not just anyone pointing you down the path—it is the Lord God, our Creator, who knows the ultimate best path for each of us.

This key leads us straight into the next key, which is David's next request: "Lead me in Your truth and teach me." I am calling this key *lead me and teach me*. David again asks the Lord, "Lead me or guide me in Your truth, in Your faithfulness. Guide me in Your uprightness and integrity. Lead me in Your justice. And in this leadership, teach me to love what You love. Teach me, oh Lord, and train me like You would train a soldier, like a singer would be instructed to sing. Oh Lord, be my guide and You teach me."

How amazing it is that our teacher is God. This word *teach* can mean to point out, as aiming the finger. I mean, imagine all of these paths in front of you, and you are saying, "God, which path should I walk down? Show me where I should go." And God takes His finger and points out the one best direction for you to walk on. God will actually teach, and He will actually point with His finger so that you have understanding of where to go and where to walk, and He will say to you, "Go down this path." These are the cries and prayers of David, and these are also the cries and prayers of you and of me.

Oh, if you hold these keys close it will be impossible to get off the divine pathway, and you will not forget the training that the Lord Himself has taught you.

Now verse 4 asks the questions, but verse 14 gives the answer. This is a promise. This is not even a key for us to use. David's testimony is, "The *secret* of the Lord or the counsel of the Lord is with those who fear Him." Now who does not want to know the counsel of the Lord or the secret of the Lord? I personally love *The Passion Translation* for this verse: "There's a private place reserved for the lovers of God, where they sit near him and receive the revelation-secrets of his promises."

Do you know that you have a reserved seat right up at the front? Right beside the Lord. And this seat—no mere man has reserved it for you, but God Himself has reserved this seat for you. It is where "He will reveal to you His innermost secrets." How do I know this?

Because David wrote about this in Psalm 25:14. And if it was true for David, then it is most certainly true for you and for me. David wrote it down so we could read this, pray this, sing this, and meet the Lord in the very same way. There is a secret place that the Lord has reserved for the lovers of God, and they will sit near Him. This means there is a company of those in close proximity; they get to sit down together with the Lord and consult—the Lord will consult with those sitting near Him, like judges sitting together, consulting together. Those sitting in their reserved seats are able to seek information or advice from the Lord, and who better to receive counsel from and consult with than God?

He has a secret, private place; it is reserved for us. This reserved seating is a place of friendship where we can literally talk with God.

It has the meaning of not just listening to God speak but actually talking things through with God, asking questions, receiving answers like you are getting a consultation from God (Strong's H5475). It's His secret place. Now when we bring in the Greek, the word isn't "secret" but "strength." However, it's interesting to note that having reverent awe (religious fear) for God connects the God-fearing, or the faithful to God's strength; typically, you'd expect that fear would bring about a state of weakness, but in here it brings *a unity* with God's strength.[1] How amazing is this? He brings us into the place of His strength.

There is one more key here—*fear the Lord*. To those who fear Him, to those who honor Him, to those who are in awe of Him, to that one possessing this key, *fear the Lord*, He will He tell His secrets.

Fear the Lord. It means to be humble, to be teachable, or to have a teachable heart, and to have a wholly reverent fear of the Lord. For the prideful man is unteachable and does not fear God. He is prideful and he cannot receive correction and teaching. However, David writes that it is the one with a humble, teachable heart, a heart filled with a holy, reverent fear for God, who can hear and receive instruction and direction from the Lord.

Oh, beloved, use these keys—number one, *show me the right path*, and number two, *teach me and lead me*. These keys will open the door to the secret place, the reserved place that God has just for you. It is the place where God will reveal His secrets and instruct us as we (pull out that third key, *fear the Lord*) have a teachable heart and a holy, reverent fear with love for God.

These are those whom God will bring into close proximity to Himself, and He will actually bring them into His place of strength, into the reserved place where we will talk with the Lord and He answers back. He will bring us into a place of friendship, and there we will consult with the Lord.

DAILY PRAYER

Oh Lord, I give my life to You. I trust You, God. I give it all to You. Oh Lord, I bring my life to You and hope in You, God. I give it all to You. Show me the right path, Lord. Point out the road for me to follow and lead me by Your truth. Teach me, for You are the God who saves.

I wrap my heart in Yours. Remember, Lord, all Your compassion whenever You look down on me with eyes of love and tender mercy. You see me, and when You think of me, see me as the one You love through Your eyes of mercy and all Your goodness.

Thank You, Lord, that there is a secret place reserved for me. You have saved a spot for me right beside Your seat. I will sit right by You, God, receiving revelation—the secrets of Your promises and I will hear You clearly.

Day 25: Write out Psalm 25

- Pray these verses out loud.

- Listen to the soaking for Psalm 25.

- Can you put yourself in the storyline of Psalm 25?

- What are you hearing in your reserved seat?

- Can you remember the keys from this psalm?

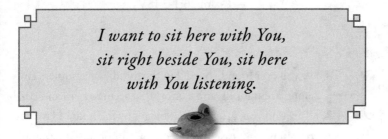

> *I want to sit here with You,*
> *sit right beside You, sit here*
> *with You listening.*

Notes

1. Joseph Meyer, formerly a Doctoral Fellow in Classical Languages and Literature at UCSB.

Day 26

Vindicate and Refine

Vindicate me, Lord, because I have walked in integrity.... Examine me, Lord, and inspect me! Test my heart and mind.
—Psalm 26:1-2 ISV

Have you ever found yourself in the middle of complete contempt, accusations, and rumors that seem to swirl and twirl all around you, growing ever bigger by the hour? Have you ever tried to present your case and tell of your innocence, but people around you were not buying it?

In Psalm 26, this is the very place where we find David. Yet again, he finds himself hated and accused, with a trail of slander, rumors, and lies spreading all throughout the land.

Although we do not have the exact timing when this psalm was penned, we do find David in great anguish calling out to God for vindication. Most commentaries agree that Saul was probably the perpetrator of these slanderous lies. Now, the *Matthew Henry Commentary* states:

It is probable that David penned this psalm when he was persecuted by Saul and his party, who, to give some colour to their unjust rage, represented him as a very bad man, and falsely accused him of many high crimes and misdemeanors, dressed him up in the skins of wild beasts that they might bait him.[1]

Can you even imagine someone hating you enough to spread such malicious lies? And then to wrap you in the skins of wild beats as bait? I had to actually read that a couple of times before I understood the meaning of that sentence. Now, the Matthew Henry Commentary does not tell us how he might have escaped this fate—but we simply know that he did. So the one who was the king and also the judge in the land, Saul, was still completely against David, filled with contempt, hate, and jealousy of this one warrior. You might say Saul wanted the very memory of David wiped out of the book, and he did all that he could possibly do as king to make this happen.

There was nothing that David could do or say that would convince Saul or his army or anyone else looking upon him that he was innocent. So David did what he always does best. He turned to God and God alone. Spurgeon says it so beautifully: "The sweet singer of Israel appears before us in this Psalm as one enduring reproach; in this he was the type of the great Son of David, and is an encouraging example to us to carry the burden of slander to the throne of grace."[2]

David appealed to the throne of grace and did not make his appeal to mere men but to God alone. He turned yet again to the supreme Judge. Right here lies our first key—*appeal to the throne of grace*. There is one God and one name who can and will deliver the righteous, and that is the Lord. Notice in this psalm David did not lift his cause to people, or friends, or peers—he went straight to the only name that he knew would deliver him. He appealed to the One sitting upon the throne of grace. Should we find ourselves in a similar situation, this is the key we want to use—*appeal to the throne of grace*.

David prays, "Vindicate me, oh my Lord." He is crying out, "God, You be the One who pronounces Your judgement upon my life." Now that is an extremely bold prayer, but David knew in the depths of his heart that he was walking before the Lord in full integrity. So he prayed in full confidence, "Vindicate me. Judge me."

Now we have seen this in several different psalms; however, David does not go back to a previous psalm and repeat his prayer. He actually makes a bookmark moment of the present time of accusation and he writes about it and sings this song to God in this same timeframe. He declares his devotion to God in this new season and he writes of his heart's resolve to love God whatever the cost.

Here lies another key, and I am calling it *resolve*. Oh, pick up this key and resolve in your heart right here and now that no matter what the circumstance, no matter what the accusation—be able to say, "This is my resolve. I am taking this key, *resolve*. I have settled this issue in my heart, and I resolve to love God and trust Him alone through every season and every trial that I walk through. I will make a bookmark moment right here—to resolve and testify again that I trust the Lord, right here and right now. I love the Lord and I walk before Him in complete truth."

Now, if you have ever heard, "Never waste a good trial," this is exactly what David did. He asked God to act as lawgiver or judge or governor in his life. He is saying, "God, rule, govern, and be the judge in my life. God, I am calling upon You to decide this controversy" (Strong's H8199).

Along with his cry to God for complete vindication, he also prays, "Examine me, O Lord, and prove me." This is a bold prayer when one needs God to step in with vindication. David prays, "Test me and prove me, try me like the gold. Look closely at my heart and examine it." God, see if my heart is not completely Yours."

When we bring in the Greek, the first verb means "to test," and the second phrase is literally, "burn my kidneys and my heart." I think the imagery is that his entire being is being engulfed in God's cleansing flame so that all that remains is pure.[3]

David is so sure of his faithful walk before the Lord that he cries out to God to not only vindicate and judge him, but, "Examine me closer, and try me seven times in the fire to reveal that my heart is like gold. Lord, ask me the hard questions, prove me even through adversity to prove that my faith is sure. My heart is set upon You."

These are very courageous prayers. This truly is the psalm of not wasting a good trial. For we have this invitation to ask God for vindication but also, in the very same breath, "God, prove me like the gold, seven times in the fire, and You will see, oh God, that from the core of my being I am faithful to You alone."

David says, "I don't sit with the people who just pretend to like You or pretend before man to serve You. I don't sit with those who are pretending and being false in their walk with You, Lord."

Can you imagine David being in this great controversy with Saul? He had one person to go to and that was the Lord. The only person who could 100 percent vindicate David was God.

This psalm would have been a song that he sang. Spurgeon calls it, "A solemn appeal to the just tribunal of the heart searching God, warranted by the circumstances of the writer, so far as regarded the particular offences with which he was wrongly charged. Worried and worn out by the injustice of men, the innocent spirit flies from its false accusers to the throne of Eternal Right."[4]

David actually makes it personal. He does two things. Number one, he prays, "God examine me, test me, prove me, try my heart. You are the heart searching God, so in this season—when I actually did nothing wrong and I have right standing before You, I am clean before You—God, I want You to examine and prove and try my heart." David makes this season about his *own heart* before God.

The second thing that David does is he sings, "Your loving kindness is before my eyes." This is quite miraculous; he doesn't dwell on all the anger and the false accusation. He does not dwell on the negative and the bitterness. He actually says, "Before my eyes I will put the loving kindness of God. I'm going to dwell on the mercy, the loving kindness and the passion of God."

This is such a great lesson for all of us. Let's invite the Lord to come examine our hearts, our motives, and our thoughts. Then, instead of our focus being on the negativity, let's put the Word of God in front of us. Let's put the loving kindness, the tender mercy, the goodness of God, our own righteous Judge, the One who actually can defend and vindicate us—let's put this amazing God front and center in our mind and heart.

David understood that walking before the Lord with a true godly character actually is inward and it's outward. It is inward because God sees all. He sees our thoughts. It is outward because all of mankind can see our heart responses.

God is always wanting to perfect that which man cannot see. I love how David makes this trial about himself. Some people have their miseries and their sorrows and their sins ever before their eyes, but David put God's loving kindness before his eyes—that became his focus.

This is our final key—*the goodness of God*. Oh beloved, take this key and set it before all that you do. So that in every season, and at every turn, our focus is the goodness of God.

Then, we can be radically attacked, we can have lies spreading about us, we can be falsely accused, and we can do what David did. He shows us right here the outcome of using these keys and keeping our focus and our heart in the right place. We can still be radically, passionately in love with God. Right in the middle of every negative, false narrative that tries to come our way, we can use these keys that David used, and our landing place is the goodness of God. Psalm 26 shows us that men's words and thoughts about us do not have to overcome our devotion and passion for God.

Can we sing the song of David, "Vindicate me, oh my Lord, for I lean on You. Come refine me. Know my heart, prove my mind and my thoughts. Would You test me and prove me like gold?"

David ended this song like he does so many, with his resolve. Can we do that too? In this age of bullying and all the social media bullying in the world, can we have the resolve of David?

Give God permission to examine you. Don't let your thoughts and your heart go to the negative place, but set the goodness and kindness of God ever before you. Have a resolve to trust the Lord. I feel every single one of us in seasons of our life can identify with what David was going through in Psalm 26.

So no matter what slander may arise, some might not ever face it, but can your resolve be, "I will trust God"? You will wholeheartedly love Him in the midst of any negative swirl. Can we all say, "Examine me and prove me and make me like the gold"?

DAILY PRAYER

Vindicate me, oh my Lord, for I lean on You. Lord, would You come refine me, know my thoughts, prove my mind and my heart, for Your loving kindness is before my eyes and I have walked in Your truth. So when I come before You I come ever clean, singing songs of thanksgiving, songs of Your wonders. I love the habitation of Your house. I love the place Your glory dwells, this place of dazzling glory and majestic splendor and the light of Your presence. Oh Lord, I will love You will my whole heart.

Day 26: Write out Psalm 26

- This week, say this psalm out loud.
- Turn it into your prayer.
- Write this psalm down.
- Decree this psalm over your life.
- Can you remember the keys from this psalm?

> *Come, refine me. Know my thoughts.
> Prove my mind and my heart.*

NOTES

1. Matthew Henry, *Matthew Henry Bible Commentary* (Psalm 26:1-5), Christianity.com, https://www.christianity.com/bible/commentary.php?com=mh&b=19&c=26.

2. Charles Spurgeon, *The Treasury of David*, "Psalm 26, Title," https://archive.spurgeon.org/treasury/treasury.php.

3. Joseph Meyer, formerly a Doctoral Fellow in Classical Languages and Literature at UCSB.

4. Spurgeon, *The Treasury of David*, "Psalm 26, verse 1."

Day 27

The Battle
and the Beauty

*The Lord is my light and my salvation—whom shall I fear? The Lord
is the stronghold of my life—of whom shall I be afraid? ...One thing I
ask from the Lord, this only do I seek: that I may dwell in the house of
the Lord all the days of my life, to gaze on the beauty of the Lord and
to seek him in his temple. ...I remain confident of this: I will
see the goodness of the Lord in the land of the living.*
—Psalm 27:1,4,13 NIV

I have sung Psalm 27:4 in many prayer services and worship services. There are songs written from this Scripture. There are paintings that were painted by an artist moved by this verse. There are
books written from this one verse. I was most familiar with the first
verse and also verse 4. I mean, honestly, who does not know Psalm
27:4? It is many people's life verse. It is the "this one thing" verse.

These verses pluck our heart strings and draw us deeper into worship and intimacy. But as I began to sing and study each psalm as a
whole—I found that David took his worship to the battle field. This
is how David fought his battles. In the middle of the battle, almost

each and every time, he began to remember the beauty of God, the power of God, the kindness of God, and as his eyes in the natural may have been looking upon a throng of wicked men coming against him, the eyes of David's heart were inwardly remembering the beauty of God and the feeling of complete peace when he was in God's presence.

I believe this psalm is for the battle. It is filled with the language of war, and then suddenly a passionate decree of *this one thing*. I think Psalm 27 takes us from the battle to the beauty, and we actually need to read verses 1 through 4 as a complete thought. For in this psalm, David finds himself in battle yet again. So when he is actually writing, "The Lord is my light and salvation," David wrote this song in a season of great trouble. Many believe he wrote this before he was actually king. We see a picture of where his heart was. It was not about being king or the greatest of warriors. *This one thing* was not set upon Samuel's prophecy and anointing on his life; it was on *this one thing*.

The *New Cambridge Bible Commentary* writes, "Psalm 27 is an example of the honest dialogue of faith characteristic of the psalmists in the face of opposition. ...It exhibits military language...and imagery of light...asks for instruction...and may relate to false accusation."[1] If you are in a war, this is your psalm. It will help you fight with confidence, yet it kindles a heart that is tender, full of devotion for the Lord alone.

He begins Psalm 27 with a declaration: "The Lord is my light and my salvation." He is saying, "God I can see clearly only because of You. You are like the sun breaking into the darkest of dawn at the start of a brand new day. It might have been dark all around, but You, oh Lord, are my light and I am able to see clearly." Here lies our first key for Psalm 27—*the Lord is my light and salvation.*

David firmly believed that God was his only light and his salvation. Have you ever pondered the fact that there is only one God who is able to give to a mere man the gift of salvation? No person or judge, president or earthly king can give salvation to man. It comes from God.

"David was a skilled, experienced warrior and must have been a man of impressive physical strength. Nevertheless, he looked to the Lord as the strength of his life."[2] He did not just sing about God being his strength; God *was* his strength. He firmly declared it and sang it throughout his life. David picked up this key—*the Lord is my light.* He was saying, "The Lord is my liberty. He alone is my deliverance, and He is my safety."

We need this key as much as David did. We can pick it up and declare it aloud. The Lord is our light. The Lord is our salvation. David put his complete confidence in the strength of God. He writes, "He keeps me from being slain, and God is also the strength of my weak and frail life." This is something that we also must embrace. This is who God was to David and this is who God *is* to us. "Nowhere else in the Old Testament is the Lord referred to as *my light.* Because the psalmist has found God as light, salvation, and strength, there is no cause for fear or terror. His serenity is not conditioned by outward circumstances but is unconditional."[3]

Then David sings out, "Whom shall I fear? Of whom shall I be afraid?" He is asking himself this real question. Almost as if to say there is *no* reason to fear, because God is and always shall be my light. He is my salvation. This is our second key—*whom shall I fear?* Ask yourself this question, and may you come to the same conclusion that David did—there is no one to fear.

In this very first verse, right at the very beginning, he is declaring that he will triumph over his enemies. He is declaring, "If God be for me, who can be against me? Why should I be fearful, though my enemies want to come upon me and kill my flesh?" He said, "They stumbled and they fell." The enemies and the hosts that had surrounded David were so confounded and weakened that they could not continue the battle.

He makes this decree; He sings out his song. He picks up his key—*the Lord is my light and my salvation*. Then he follows that decree with a question that he has already answered in his heart—*whom shall I fear*? I will fear no man; the Lord is my light and salvation. In the midst of this verse, David looks and sees his enemies stumble and fall. He begins to trust God above all else. Even though there was a numerous host wanting to surround David, through their daring attempts and though they waged war against him, he was steady in his heart with this key and this one sentence: "*Whom shall I fear?*" Can we ask ourselves the very same question? Who is there that we fear? Because there is no fear needed when God is our light and salvation, our strength, and He rescues us time and time again.

David was trusting not in those fighting with him, not in his own strength, but there was a host of Heaven that was David's constant protection. Oh, the host who is against us cannot hurt us if the Lord of hosts is protecting us. When David uses the word *host*, that means there were throngs of them; there were so many that David could not even begin to count them, and they were all against him. Here is his testimony. He pulled out that key and sang *whom shall I fear*? They cannot hurt us when the host of Heaven protects us.

We need to use these words as our weapon. We can pull out this key, *whom shall I fear*? Suddenly in this battle, we find ourselves in verse 4. We are in the core of the battle when we take a sudden turn. It is like we have a new scene. But it is not a new scene. This is part of the battle plan. We find David in the most beautiful and throne-centered worship: "One thing I ask of the Lord—this one thing I seek."

Start singing Psalm 27:4 before the enemy has retreated and before your sword is put down. David shows us right here how to fight our battles. Verses 2 and 3 show us that this beautiful portion of Scripture *belongs* right in the middle of the battle. God is right in the midst of your battle. Here lies our third key—*this one thing*. Three very simple words—*this one thing*. Now, what David didn't say: "One thing I ask of the Lord is that I would have a really strong army to defeat these enemies."

I began to ask myself, "What do I ask God for when I'm in the midst of the battle?" What do you ask God for when you are in the midst of the battle? David said *one thing*. I asked the Lord for this one thing. I desire one thing. I desire You, God. I desire sweet fellowship with You.

He wanted to live right there. He wanted the wars to cease, and he wanted to be in the house of God gazing upon the beauty of God. He saw his protection right here. For the sanctuary was to David a place of worship, but in this psalm it is also his place of refuge. He found beauty and refuge in the sanctuary. God defended and protected David as effectually as if he had placed and hidden David in the innermost recesses of His tabernacle.[4]

He just wants to spend his life beholding the beauty of the Lord. It is almost as if he was saying, "There's no greater thing that I want to do in my life. I want my heart and my mind to meditate and sing about the goodness and greatness of God. I want to gaze, not a passing glance, but I want to look closely at You and begin to see more and more about You." He desires to look upon the splendor and beauty of the Lord—the kindness, pleasantness, and delightfulness of the Lord. *Gaze* can mean "to see God, sometimes used of the real sight of the divine presence" (Strong's H2372). Can you imagine? Face to face with God?

David's passion was to gaze on the beauty of God; then that gaze turned into this unquenchable desire to be with God all of his days. It was like a fire that began to burn stronger and hotter and grew within David the more he would look and behold, spend time in His presence, just looking at Him through the Scriptures and any added revelation that God gave to David.

And remember when you read and pray these verses—David was in the middle of battle, watching a host of enemies fall before him, taking out those keys, *the Lord is my light and salvation*, and *whom shall I fear*. Oh, I can just hear him singing and praying these words out loud. So when you read Psalm 27, read verses 1, 2, 3, and then 4. They all go together. Don't just focus on the devotional; David had the devotional right in the middle of war, right in the middle of enemies.

Though the host encamped against David, his heart did not fear; though war rose against him, he pulled out that key—*the Lord is my light and salvation*. Then he pulled out the second key—*whom shall I fear*? And that leads us right to our third key—*this one thing*. Can you just hear him singing out, "This one thing I've asked the

Lord"? He gained confidence minute by minute as his gaze was on the beauty of God, the power of God, the goodness of God.

He made his declaration at the very beginning—the Lord is my light and my salvation, whom shall I fear? The Lord is the strength of my life, of whom shall I be afraid? He walks us through that battle scene and then shows us how to fight. Oh, God, my confidence is in this one thing. David's confidence was in the knowledge of God. God is my light. God is my strength.

We always take Psalm 27:4 and we make it worship. It is worship, but it's worship as we remember the battle. It's worship before you know the final outcome of the battle.

If we walk through really hard times, this is our psalm. This is our declaration of who God is in our life and our declaration that those enemies and the host that is against us, they will stumble and fall. This is my confidence. God is my light. God is my salvation. Whom shall I fear?

Can you just hear David praying, "I want to gaze on Your beauty, God. I want my meditation on Your beauty to actually turn into inquiry and a seeking heart after You in a greater way. God, I want to see You more"?

So where are you today? Where is your trouble? The good thing about the Psalms is they give us many songs to sing over our trouble.

David brings his devotion and his desire to see God right in his trouble. This is one of the things I've been so impacted by as I sing through the Psalms. There is no separation.

David brings his, "I love You, I love You, God"—he brings that love song to the battlefield. He brings his declaration and his gazing on the beauty of God right into real life. "God, I just want to know You. I want to see You."

I want to encourage you to bring Psalm 27 into every area that you are in a battle or you feel trouble right around the corner. Let this push you forward into the beauty realm of God. That is what is going to sustain us in shaking times. Our intimacy will be our strength. Our knowledge of God will be our portion.

Pick up these keys, *the Lord is my strength* and *whom shall I fear?* It is like the more you use these keys, the more confident you shall become. You will find that there is a heart cry just like David had of *this one thing*. I desire to gaze on Your beauty, Your glory, Your kindness, Your power—this will overtake your heart and mind so that all through the battle, you will be led straight to beauty.

Now there is a promise right at the end of this incredible psalm: "I would have fainted unless I believed I would see the goodness of God in the land of the living." *I will see the goodness of God in my life today*, right here and right now. This was David's promise—it was his exclamation mark as he brought this psalm to completion.

The land of the living is today. We are alive and breathing right here. It is not mostly about eternity. It is now. Can we do this today? Can we look for the goodness of God? Even if you are in the middle of a battle, bring in the beauty. Keep this psalm on your lips and look around—look for the goodness of God today.

DAILY PRAYER

Lord, whom shall I fear? You are my light and my salvation. You are my fortress, protecting me from danger. You are the very strength of my life. Oh God, whom shall I fear? When the wicked, even my enemies and my foes, come against me they stumble and fall. Though a host would come against me my heart shall not fear; through war break out against me, I will not be afraid for You are my very strength.

Right in the middle of the battle, this is my heart's cry. For it is this One thing I ask of You, Lord; it's the only thing I seek. This is the only thing I want, and I desire. I want to see Your beauty. I want to see Your eyes. I want to gaze into Your eyes of fire. Lord, I want to live in Your house all of my days. I want to gaze upon Your beauty. Oh, to see Your beauty in Your sanctuary.

You will hide me in Your sanctuary. You will place me high upon a rock. You will set me high upon an immovable rock.

Oh, to be face to face with God as I rest in Your presence, You are my only help. You are the very strength of my life. Oh, my heart beats for one thing.

Day 27: Write out Psalm 27

- This week, say this psalm out loud.
- Turn it into your prayer.
- Write this psalm down.
- Decree this psalm over your life.
- Where do you see God's goodness at work today?
- Can you remember the keys from this psalm?

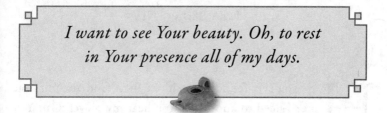

> *I want to see Your beauty. Oh, to rest in Your presence all of my days.*

Notes

1. Brueggemann, *New Cambridge Bible Commentary*, 139.

2. David Guzik, "Psalm 27: The Seeking, Waiting Life Rewarded," The Enduring Word Bible Commentary, https://enduringword .com/bible-commentary/psalm-27.

3. Pfeiffer and Harrison, *The Wycliffe Bible Commentary*, 505.

4. Saint Robert Bellarmine, *A Commentary on the Book of Psalms*, 115.

Day 28

The Divine Shift

To you, Lord, I call; You are my Rock, do not turn a deaf ear to me. ...
Praise be to the Lord, for he has heard my cry for mercy. The Lord
is my strength and my shield; my heart trusts in him,
and he helps me. My heart leaps for joy.
—Psalm 28:1,6-7 NIV

Have you ever found yourself praying, "God, do You hear me? I need to know that You hear my prayer. Can You hear my sound? Can You hear my cry?" Have you ever felt so alone? If you have ever felt so weak because you simply needed to know beyond a shadow of a doubt that God indeed heard your prayer, well, this may just be your psalm. This is right where we find David in Psalm 28. He is crying these very same words, feeling the very same way. He needs to know that God has heard his cry.

Psalm 28 lets us peek into David's prayer life. We find him crying out to God with an earnest pleading, that inner groan that says, "God, if You don't break in, I feel as if my life will end." I love *The Passion Translation* for this first verse: "I'm pleading with you, Lord, help me! Don't close your ears to my cry, for you're my defender. If you continue to remain aloof and refuse to answer me, I might as well give up and die."

Now, that is pretty dire. We are not certain the exact timing of this psalm; however, Derek Kidner writes in his Psalms commentary, "The situation is probably illness or deep despair and the fear is not a dread of death, as such, but of death with unmerited disgrace."[1] David wrote Psalm 28 in dire circumstances—so dire and so stressful that if God didn't break in, he felt that death was at his doorstep. David needed to know that God heard and was not silent and distant.

> [Psalm 28] is another of those "songs in the night" of which
> the pen of David was so prolific. The thorn at the breast of
> the nightingale was said by the old naturalists to make it sing;
> David's griefs made him eloquent in holy psalmody.[2]

We left Psalm 27 in a very high place of declaring that God works *today*, while we are alive, not just a future tense of eternity, but God is a strength and hope now. Then, with one flip of the page, we find David again in complete dire need of his Rock. I love how he has no trouble in writing about his needs. He starts out yet again in complete need of God, and he is not ashamed to admit his weakness. He pours out his heart in the next few verses, and then we see a divine shift.

We have seen this in many of David's psalms. He begins in complete weakness, failure, or despair, and his prayer life, his ability to honestly and sincerely talk to the Lord, always leads him to the knowledge that God hears and God will act on his behalf. He does not turn to man for help. He does not turn to family for help. He does what he does best—he turns to his only Rock and asks for help. Here lies our first key—*help*. Just lift up that cry. *Help, help, oh God.* Just be as honest and vulnerable with the Lord as you can possibly be. Tell Him what is happening as you lift up this key—*help*. This key, this honest plea in weakness of *help,* is the very on-ramp for the divine shift.

There is another key here—*You are my rock*. Right in the middle of our honest pleas for help, let us do what David did and just state the fact that God is our Rock. Spurgeon writes, "The immutable Jehovah is our *rock,* the immovable foundation of all our hopes and our refuge in time of trouble: we are fixed in our determination to flee to him as our stronghold in every hour of danger."[3]

Use this key, *You are my rock,* as a reminder of who God is for you, even before you feel this. It is truth. Say this out loud. Pick up this key; use it every day to remind your heart—You are my rock.

> David said that the Lord was his Rock—his foundation, his stability, his security. "It is a remarkable fact that in all the Old Testament literature, 'rock' is reserved as a figure of Deity... never for man."[4]

Oh beloved, take out these keys—*help* and *You are my rock*. In the middle of a cry for help, remind your heart of this truthful statement. *You are my rock*. Then watch the heart begin to realize the truth. You are not alone. God hears that tender and faint cry, *help*. You are already on the Rock. He never left. The Rock did not move.

Then, the divine switch that is so familiar in the psalms penned by David—his pleadings, his woes, and his constant sorrows shift to faith and rejoicing. We find this shift in verse 6: "Praise be to the Lord; He has heard my cry for mercy." This does not even sound like the same person praying as at the beginning of the psalm because suddenly truth has its perfect way in David's heart.

Oh, how miraculous. The heart suddenly understands the reality that God hears. What is even more wonderful is this *same* shift can work in our lives also. We can sing and pray our way to faith just like David does. We can sing our way to hope and victory even if we feel like our whole world is caving in. When we will sing and pray out loud the words that David prayed, this supernatural shift from fear to faith has its perfect way within us, just like we saw it have its way within David.

In verse 6, there is a glorious turn into praise. This song of praise begins to arise as faith has overtaken a once fearful heart. This is a perfect picture of starting weak and in need but continuing an ongoing conversation with God. Never stop using that first key—God, *help*. By using the words David prayed, that same divine shift from fear to faith will also take place within us. These words are powerful, even when David writes from the place of weakness. Suddenly, those living words begin to have their full effect as David sings and prays. Those dire claws of fear let go and David is engulfed in steady, courageous faith. The perils of fear once again loose their grip on the psalmist who sings and prays his meditations to God.

"Blessed be the Lord, because He has heard the voice of my supplication." David's testimony in song is, "God has heard my cry." He answers the very pleas and requests that he sought after in verse 1. He answered his own prayer. He now has no doubt that his cry has made its way right to the very throne of God.

David has the attention of God and he is sure of it. This is no longer a fearful David; the divine shift has happened and there is an assuredness within his innermost being that God hears. Right now, he knows he is in the company of God and His heavenly host, and David's voice and sound have made their way straight to God.

This is where we take Psalm 28 and make it personal. We don't have to start the prayer strong; we can begin weak, even with a feeling of distance. Here lies our third key—*He has heard my cry*. Say this out loud many times a day. This is truth. God has heard my cry. Take this key and use it often. Say it over and over, sing it out. God has heard. My cry has made its way into the ears and heart of God. This is the truth. God has heard your cry.

David's divine shift can also be ours. We can take these very words as our own. Take out this key, *He has heard my cry*. Open that door and keep on going. God has heard my voice. The Lord has heard my sound. He has heard my singing. God has heard my thundering sound, and not only has He heard, He intends to answer. This same strengthening knowledge will also make its divine shift within us.

We can start weak, but if we just keep the conversation going, we will be the ones shouting, *God has heard my cry*. He has heard even my whisper. My safety, my praise is that God hears my cry.

David starts with pleas, but he ends in absolute confidence. His song is his declaration. "The Lord is my strength. The Lord is my force, my security, He is my praise. He is my boldness. God is my might and power."

Here we find new confidence. I am helped because I am surrounded; I am protected. I have help all around me, and this causes my heart to greatly rejoice. So I will praise. I will worship, and with my song I totally surrender to the One who is my protector and my strength.

Psalm 28 is our invitation to change our mindset; He hears, and He is with us now. When this is alive in our heart and mind, we will actually start living life like it is.

We can bear anything and everything because God is our strength. David adds his voice to the testimony of countless others who have found help as their heart trusts in God. This whole-hearted trust can be ours also.

DAILY PRAYER

Praise be to the Lord; He has heard my cry for mercy. Praise be to the Lord; He has heard my cry for help. Lord, You are my strength and You are my shield. My heart trusts in You. I will lean upon You. And every single time I cry, You help me. You don't leave me alone; You don't leave my calls for help unheard.

Thank You, Lord, You hear my cries and You answer them. Thank You for Your constant attentive listening ears. Thank You for Your heart as a Father and a tender shepherd to reach down and bear me up in Your strong arms.

I will praise You. I will tell of Your goodness. I will make my testimony known before the people. You make my heart so glad.

Oh Lord, You are mighty and You watch over and guard Your chosen ones. Oh, Your watchful eyes are always upon me; like a shepherd, You lead me. Like a shepherd, You go on before me and You carry me in Your arms. To You I call, oh Lord, to You I call, my Rock. You are my immovable, secure Rock whom I may call on in days of trouble. I will praise You, oh Lord. You hear my cry and You answer. Thank You.

Day 28: Write out Psalm 28

- This week, say this psalm out loud.
- Turn it into your prayer.
- Write this psalm down.
- Decree this psalm over your life.
- Be brave—sing it out loud.
- Can you remember the keys from this psalm?

> *Praise be to the Lord.*
> *He has heard my cry for mercy.*
> *He has heard my cry for help.*

Notes

1. Kidner, *Psalms*, 140.

2. Charles Spurgeon, *The Treasury of David*, "Psalm 28, Title and Subject," https://archive.spurgeon.org/treasury/treasury.php.

3. Ibid., "Psalm 28, verse 1."

4. David Guzik, "Psalm 28: Praise from Prayer Heard and Answered," The Enduring Word Bible Commentary, https://enduringword.com/bible-commentary/psalm-28.

Week 5

Day 29

This Is the One

*Give to the Lord, you heavenly beings, give to the Lord glory and
strength. Give to the Lord the glory of His name; worship the Lord
in holy splendor. The voice of the Lord is over the waters; the God of
glory thunders; the Lord is over many waters. The voice of the Lord
sounds with strength; the voice of the Lord—with majesty. The voice
of the Lord breaks the cedars...The voice of the Lord flashes like flames
of fire. The voice of the Lord shakes the wilderness...and in His temple
everyone says, "Glory!" The Lord sits enthroned above the flood, the
Lord sits as King forever. The Lord will give strength to His people.*
—Psalm 29

Just as the eighth Psalm is to be read by moonlight, when the
stars are bright, as the nineteenth needs the rays of the rising
sun to bring out its beauty, so this can be best rehearsed beneath
the black wing of tempest, by the glare of the lightning, or amid that
dubious dusk which heralds the war of elements. The verses march to
the tune of thunderbolts. God is everywhere conspicuous, and all the
earth is hushed by the majesty of his presence.[1]

I grew up in the Midwest, right in the middle of Kansas on the
edge of tornado alley. In fact, I have been through three different

tornados and three microbursts. Now, all of those are beyond my ability to even try to put into words—the sounds, the power, and the fear that overtook me every single time. As a young girl in Belvue, Kansas, I remember that first tornado—one probably never forgets the first tornado. My mom, Penny, my little sis, and I were at home. Dad must have been at work, and it began to rain and thunder. There are lots of different kinds of thunder. There is the beautiful rolling thunder that seems to roll from one side of the sky to the other. There is the rumbling thunder, where it is like a rumbling coming from all parts of the sky. Then there is that thunder crack that tells you, "Get inside, the storm is near."

There is nothing like the sound of thunder as it cracks in the sky or the sound of lightning as it strikes the earth or the peals of lightning traveling on its course through the sky. I remember that night—the rain, the wind blowing and howling. I remember the sound of lightning, the bolts of thunder cracking all across the sky and all throughout our house. It felt like it was right over our heads. In fact one summer a lightning bolt struck our front patio and left a crack from one side to the other. That was a deafening sound and I remember it every time I go back to the farm. It was a moment that we all decided to let God leave His mark on our front patio so we never fixed it.

Then, there was calm. It was an *eerie* calm. If you have ever heard the saying "the calm before the storm," well, that is what happens before a tornado. My mom ran to my sis, picked her up, and grabbed my hand at the same time. We ran down those basement stairs lick-ety-split (if you are from Kansas, you know that means very, very fast), and we all huddled in the corner. As a small girl, the sounds of those winds were deafening. If you have ever seen the movie *Tornado*, that was pretty true to life. We huddled in that corner until all the winds were calm and then we huddled there some more. We all made it through our first tornado.

In the fourth grade our family moved to Wamego, and there I experienced my second and third tornado; neither one of them were fun either. I did not get any braver because I had been through one already. Many years later, I remember sitting on the back deck talking with my dad. It was July 3, because the carnival was in town. We had just had our first ever cousins' reunion with tables and chairs for 40 people set up in the backyard. We were sitting out on the rails of the front deck, and in an instant those winds picked up from 10 miles an hour to 80 miles an hour. It nearly threw my dad and me off the deck. Now, sometimes you get the storm, then the calm before the storm, and other times you just get the tornado. My Dad and I ran to the back yard and began to break down the tables. My boys were yelling from the house, "Mom, you are going to die!" I yelled back, "Get to the basement."

I remember looking over and seeing the wind literally pick up my sister, Penny, and throw her into the house. Things happened so fast. I ran to help her up and yelled, "Get to the basement." And my dad, fearless as he is, said, "I'm going to check the horses," to which my sister answered, "I'm going with Dad." They hopped in the truck and I hopped to the basement with the Meyer boys. We sat down in that old basement—those walls were so old. This house was over 100 years old, and those walls were made of stone on top of stone. I remember praying, "Help, Lord. Keep these walls strong." One of our boys prayed, "Lord, take care of BooCat." Yes, BooCat was somewhere out in the middle of a tornado. Oh, how the winds howled, and oh, how the house creaked. Those winds sounded like a freight train coming right at us.

However, we all survived. My dad and sister got back. The horses were OK and BooCat came running in the house drenched with rain and meowing up a storm—but all were safe.

So when I read, pray, and sing through Psalm 29, "The voice of the Lord is over the waters; the God of glory thunders," I can go right back to those Midwest storms and have a slight understanding of the sound, the power, and the glory of God—our Creator, the one who created the most powerful entities in the cosmos, in the universe, in the earth, in the sea. The One who created the most powerful sounds in all creation—He is over them all. He is *more* powerful than them *all*.

When David began to pen Psalm 29, he most lightly was in the fields tending his sheep, as a storm came over the back hills of Bethlehem. Maybe the storm started with some rumbling in the distance. I can close my eyes and see David, who would have known where all the best caves and caverns were because he lived out in those fields. As the distant rumble of thunder began to echo across the Judean hills, maybe at that first sight of lightning, David gathered his sheep into a safe cavern, watching the storm begin to play its musical rhythms and sounds all across the sky. Maybe he watched the lightning make its shining appearance all throughout the heavens.

Then at some point with the rumbling of the thunder, he may have pulled out his pen and scroll and begun to record this storm as it danced across the sky. Maybe those first couple of rumbles and lightning, he saw as Heaven's call to worship, for David started this psalm calling all heavenly beings to come worship the Lord. As the storm begins to build, David continues to write and record the unfolding storm, and he sees God throughout the whole thunder and light show.

Or maybe David was listening and watching the storm unfold, yet thinking back to Moses, when Moses was invited to a meeting with God.

> *So on the third day, in the morning, there was thunder and lightning, and a thick cloud on the mountain, and the sound of an exceedingly loud trumpet. All the people who were in the camp trembled. ...Now Mount Sinai was completely covered in smoke because the Lord had descended upon it in fire, and the smoke ascended like the smoke of a furnace, and the whole mountain shook violently. When the sound of the trumpet grew louder and louder, Moses spoke, and God answered him with a voice* [some translations say "thunder"] (Exodus 19:16,18-19).

Maybe as David began to record this powerful storm, he remembered the invitation that Moses received to meet with God in the middle of a lightning storm. Maybe David even considered himself right there, meeting God face to face, and therefore began his call to worship starting with the heavenly beings.

Here lies our first key—*call to worship.* I love how David is witnessing this giant storm and the first thing out of his mouth is a call to worship. David calls all, above and below, in Heaven and on the earth, "Come, give to the Lord the glory of His name, the splendor and honor of His name. Give Him all you have and all you are.

Worship the Lord, honor Him in all of His majesty and beauty, in all of His holiness and strength."

Then maybe it started to rain, the rolling thunder beginning to slowly approach closer and closer to where David and his sheep had taken refuge. As the rain began to come down stronger and stronger, faster and faster, David, seeing God in the storm, sang out, "The voice of the Lord is over the waters." The sound, the noise, the thunder of the Lord is over the waters. David Guzik writes, "His authoritative voice proclaims His dominion over the waters. This is the first of seven descriptions of the voice of the Lord in this psalm. Each one emphasizes the idea of the strength and authority of God expressed through His words."[2]

Then, maybe David hears the sound of a thunderbolt—a sound more than a rumble, but a bolting thunder crack as it echoes throughout the sky. David again writes down and sings out, "The God of glory thunders." The closest thing that David has to compare the voice of God to is the thunderbolt that peals throughout the heavens. Spurgeon writes, "The thunder is not only poetically but instructively called 'the voice of God,' since it peels from on high; it surpasses all other sounds, it inspires awe, it is entirely independent of man. ...No sound more calculated to inspire reverent awe than the roar of the storm."[3]

Here lies our second key. I am calling this key, *listen*. Oh, when you hear the mighty waters or the crashing waves, can you say to yourself, "Listen to His voice. Listen to His sound"? If you find yourself at the edge of the sea or by the mighty waterfalls, can you *listen* and say to yourself, "God is over the mighty waters"? Take some time and just stand. Just stand in one place without talking and listen to the sound. Listen to the mighty thunderous roar of water and say to yourself, "This is what God sounds like."

David is witness to the voice and the power of God expressed through every vibration, every thunderclap, all the winds, and all the thunderous sounds of rain. Right here, we can make this personal. For God not only thunders over the sea, sending forth the strikes of lightning, but this is our God who thunders over our lives and our family and our destiny. Do you ever feel like you are in a raging emotional storm? Spurgeon actually makes this verse personal, saying, "The Holy Spirit makes the divine promise to be heard above the many waters of our soul's trouble."[4] God thunders over the raging emotional storms of our lives. God is as glorious over our emotional struggles as He is glorious over the universe. The *Matthew Henry Bible Commentary* writes:

> *The voice of the Lord*, in the thunder, often *broke the cedars,* even those of Lebanon, the strongest, the stateliest. Some understand it of the violent winds which shook the cedars, and sometimes tore off their aspiring tops. Earthquakes also shook the ground itself on which the trees grew, and made *Lebanon and Sirion* to dance.[5]

The cedars of Lebanon were well known for their strength, yet the voice of God is so powerful that His voice can actually shatter these mighty trees. Again, we can imagine David watching this mighty thunderstorm, possibly seeing a lightning bolt come crashing down upon a cedar tree as it splits in two with splinters flying through the atmosphere.

At the sight and sound of such remarkable power, I can picture David bowing down, letting his pen fall to the ground and just maybe he joined the chorus of "All cry glory." I think he said, "All cry glory" over and over and over until he could once again peel himself up off the ground, slowly turning his eyes toward Heaven relating the power and majesty of the storm to the One who sits supreme as King forever.

Here lies another key—*make it personal*. Take this psalm and make it yours. God is speaking not only to David, but He is speaking and revealing His glory and mighty power for you. As you read and pray through this psalm, keep in mind He is personal. The One who thunders from Heaven is the same One who hears and answers our prayers. He will give security, boldness, and might to you and to me. Take your key, *make it personal,* and pray this Psalm over your own life: God, with His thunderous voice is over everything. He is the One who gives you and me strength for my everyday life."

God comes to us as a comfort. Saint Augustine said, "For the Lord will give strength to his people fighting against the storms and whirlwinds of this world."

Are you in a storm today? Maybe it's an emotional storm that swirls and strikes your heart like lightning striking the earth. Maybe you are a witness to a great storm that topples mighty trees and shakes everything around you. Pick up these keys, *call to worship,* stop right where you are and worship the Lord using Psalm 29. Pick up the second key: *listen,* then listen to the sounds in the middle of the wind, rain, and thunder. As you listen, know that the same God who created the storm is over the storm. Then the third key, *make it personal*. Invite the Lord in the middle of your storm. See Him as the One with power over nature as His mighty voice sounds like thunder and crashing lightning—This is the One who gives strength to you and me.

DAILY PRAYER

Oh God, remind me that You give me strength and power to walk through anything that comes my way. You are greater than any storm I will face. As I pray the very words that David prayed, Lord, show me Your almighty power, as Creator of all, Lord of All and reigning as King forever.

I join with the heavenly hosts, I join with the chorus of the mighty ones and give You glory. I give you honor. Lord, I give You all of the glory and honor due Your name. I worship You and bow down in reverence before You. And I ask, Lord, let me see You as You really are.

Open my eyes that I would understand what it means that You are clothed in all of Your splendor as if Splendor adorns You and wraps itself around You like a garment. Your Holiness is beautiful.

You appear in all of Your beauty, revealing who You are through the storm, through the shakings. I am in awe before such power and might. Oh that I would see and know Your greatness, Your beauty, Your power, and Your holiness.

God, Your voice is mighty. Your voice is over the waters. Your voice echoes above the sea. Your voice is powerful. Your voice is majestic. God, You reign as You thunder in the clouds.

Your thunder breaks the cedars. Your voice strikes like flashes of lightning. You reveal Yourself as You shake the desert and Your mighty voice makes the deer to give birth. Your voice lays the forests bare. Oh God, we come and worship You.

All in Your temple, are falling before You, each one shouting glory, glory. Lord, I join this chorus and bow before Your greatness. I surrender completely and join in the shouts of glory, glory.

For the One whose voice is over the waters, whose voice is louder than the crashing of the waves. This is the One who gives strength to me. You are the One who gives Your might to me. You bless Your people with peace. You reign as King forever.

Day 29: Write out Psalm 29

- This week, say this psalm out loud.

- Turn it into your prayer.

- Write this psalm down.

- Decree this psalm over your life.

- Be brave—sing it out loud.

- Can you write down how you picture the God of glory?

- Can you write down how You have seen God thunder over your life and give you strength?

- Can you remember the keys from this psalm?

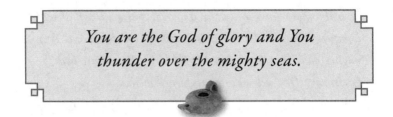

You are the God of glory and You thunder over the mighty seas.

NOTES

1. Spurgeon, *The Treasury of David*, "Psalm 29, Subject."

2. David Guzik, "Psalm 29: The Voice of the Lord in the Storm," The Enduring Word Bible Commentary, https://enduringword.com/bible-commentary/psalm-29.

3. Charles Spurgeon, *The Treasury of David*, "Psalm 29, verse 3," https://archive.spurgeon.org/treasury/treasury.php.

4. Ibid.

5. Matthew Henry, *Matthew Henry Bible Commentary* (Psalm 29:1-11, II, 2), Christianity.com, https://www.christianity.com/bible/commentary.php?com=mh&b=19&c=29.

Day 30

He Still Is

I will extol You, O Lord, for You have drawn me up, and have not caused my foes to rejoice over me O Lord my God, I cried to You, and You healed me. O Lord, You have brought up my soul from the grave; You have kept me alive, that I should not go down to the pit. ...For His anger endures but a moment, in His favor is life; weeping may endure for a night, but joy comes in the morning. ...You have turned my mourning into dancing; You have put off my sackcloth and girded me with gladness...O Lord my God, I will give thanks to You forever.
—Psalm 30:1-3,5,11-12

Wow, here we are. The last chapter and we did it! Thirty days in the Psalms. And boy, do we have an amazing psalm as we round out our last chapter. Give yourself a pat on the back. Can you think back over these last 29 chapters? Is there a psalm that you said. "This is me? This is right where I am in life." Maybe you found several psalms that you could say that about. Well, now you have the keys to pick up and use to fight any battle you face in life. That is what the Psalms do—they give us keys for battle. They give us language to have an ongoing conversation with the Lord throughout our entire lifetime.

As we jump into Psalm 30, pour yourself some coffee, get out your journal, and let's dive deep into this amazing chapter packed full of keys and promises. If you need healing in your life, if you need deliverance or restoration, if you need joy or hope, this is your psalm. David titles this psalm:

A Song at the dedication of the temple. Though the title of the psalm (as it is in the English translation) indicates it was written for the dedication of David's palace, Charles Spurgeon (and Adam Clarke) thought that it was actually written prophetically for the dedication of the temple—which David prepared for, but Solomon built.[1]

Here we have another psalm prophetically written, a joyful song of dedication for David's own palace as he peers into the future dedication of the temple that his son, Solomon, would build. He writes this psalm of dedication in *thanksgiving* for the greatness of God. His desire for the greatness of God to continue in song all throughout the ages is still happening today. This is a psalm for the seers. This is a psalm for prophetic singers, minstrels, and at the same time it is a psalm for the one who needs great healing.

Psalm 30 has impacted my own life over two thousand years *after* David wrote it. I am still able to put myself in the storyline and I want to invite you to do the same as you read and pray through Psalm 30. For God who was faithful to David will also be faithful to us. God who was great in David's life, He will be great all throughout ours.

We find some of these Scriptures in many songs, books, poems, Bible studies, and art. They have been written or painted from the very words in David's testimony. "His anger is but for a moment and

His favor is for a lifetime"—this one line is in songs that many have sung for years. We also have "Weeping may last for the night, but joy comes with the morning"—that is a very popular hymn that has been sung by multitudes. Books have been written from this one Scripture that continue to be popular and read throughout the whole world. Spurgeon writes, "Their mourning shall last but till morning. God will turn their winter's night into a summer's day, their sighing into singing, their grief into gladness, their mourning into music, their bitter into sweet, their wilderness into a paradise."[2] This is not just David's promise. This is our promise.

We also have "You have turned my mourning into dancing." There are countless songs that use this very verse along with "You have taken off my sackcloth and clothed me in gladness." I even wrote my own song, titled, "I've Got the Joy," out of this verse.

> God set my feet a dancing
> Gave me beauty for my ashes
> God set my feet a dancing
> Gave me joy for mourning.[3]

So we can see how one prophetic song began to flow like a river from generation to generation. These are the words that live on and on, filling hymn books, songbooks, and filling the hearts and mouths of many who continue to sing these words. It brings us right back to the Word of God that endures forever. It stands true throughout all generations. Here lies our first key—*be*. Be the writer. Be the singer.

Be the seer. Be the artist. What has God done in your life? Be the one to tell your own testimony. Testimony breeds faith. Where there are testimonies there is a greater measure of faith. Be the psalmist.

Put yourself in the story line and use this key, *be*. Be the one to tell the stories of the greatness of God in your life. Can you take a little time and write down some of the ways God's greatness has been revealed in your life? Can you then just take some time and tell the Lord how thankful you are for His enduring Word?

David starts this psalm off with his own personal testimony of being one breath away from the grave. He writes, "I extol" or "I lift You up, oh Lord, because You have *drawn me up*. You have helped me when I could not help myself." The King James says, "You have lifted me up." The word *lift* is a word picture of letting down a bucket into a well to draw water—"to draw out, to take out, to set free" (Strong's H1802). See a picture in your mind of David being swallowed up into the depths and God, throwing out a lifeline, or God reaching down and pulling David out of that which he could not pull himself out of. Abraham Ibn Ezre writes, "God raised him up, because David thought he was going to die."[4] Whatever sickness David was wrestling with, he felt death was sure to come.

The chorus of this psalm is, "O Lord, my God, I cried to You, and You healed me." Oh, what a promise. Oh, what a verse. I love how *The Passion Translation* reads, "O Lord, my healing God, I cried out for a miracle and You healed me!" This is our second key—*my healing God*. He is. He still is. He was God who healed David and He still is the God who heals us today. This amazing promise, this amazing key—*my healing God*—get 100 of these keys and leave them all around your home just as a reminder of who He is and what He still does today. Oh Lord, *my* healing God. He is yours and He is my healing God. Never leave this key. Put it front and center. This is a promise and it is words that endure forever. He was, He is, and He will always be our healing God—at least while we are on earth. What a joyful promise. What a reason to celebrate. He is our healing God.

There is such a tremendous promise in verse 2, "I cried to You and You healed me." We have covered so many psalms in which our simple cries reach the ear of God and He answers. David cries out; this word *cry* can mean "to ask for aid, to implore, to shout out." It is that inner groan of, "God, help" (Strong's H7768). You are my only help.

Here lies our third key—*cry out*. Yes, lift your voice. Ask God for help. Believe that He will listen and answer. Shout out. No voice is too soft, no voice is too loud, no voice asks too often. Just let your voice be heard. Don't wait; just use that key, *cry out*. You have a God just waiting to answer your cries for help. You have permission to ask for healing. Use that key, *cry out*

Then comes the testimony, the answer from David's cries. You healed me. This is not a key. *This is a promise*. God is the healer—You are our healing God. He is our physician. The word *heal* means to cure, to heal, to repair, to thoroughly make whole, restore health (Strong's H7495). God is the healer and when we cry out for a miracle, He will heal us. He will cure us. He will be our great physician. He will repair us. He will thoroughly make us whole through and through. What an incredible promise to sing. This was David's promise and testimony, and it is also our promise and testimony.

When we bring in the Greek for the word *heal*, it also can mean heal/treat/repair/cure. Contextually, its meaning could range from miraculous recovery from an illness, to psychologically restore someone's mental state, to becoming well from being sick as a result of medicine. It's fairly close in meaning to the English "heal."[5]

Spurgeon writes:

> *"Thou hast healed me,"* means, Thou hast brought me out of my distresses, hast restored my health, and rendered me safe and prosperous. Under Saul, he was frequently in the most imminent danger of his life, out of which God wonderfully brought him, which he strongly expresses by saying, *"Thou hast brought up my soul from* Hades: *thou hast kept me alive, that I should not go down to the pit."*[6]

Many times when David talks about the pit, it is in reference to the grave. God heard David's cry and pulled him out. *The Passion Translation* reads, "You brought me back from the brink of death, from the depths below. Now here I am, alive and well, fully restored!"

I found myself in Psalm 30 when I also received a great miracle. Years ago, I began to go hoarse. Now, this is a fairly big deal when you are a singer in a 24/7 House of Prayer movement. I went to the doctor and was diagnosed with acid reflux disease. My doctor had me on a daily schedule of Nexium with an endoscopy every three years. On the first scope the doctor saw that I did not have an esophageal sphincter. This is much needed in the body because it opens when you eat and swallow, allowing food to pass into your stomach, then it closes to keep all tummy acid and food from coming back up in the esophagus. Without this very needed part, I was continually going hoarse and had a continual cough. I have two different doctor reports showing exactly the same thing.

Our family moved to Santa Maria in 2015 to be a part of the Healing Rooms Apostolic Center. The testimonies of healing that have happened from this ministry are quite amazing. In fact, they were given two different awards from the city of Santa Maria for "Best Natural Healing." This was given to the Healing Room directors, Rick and Lori Taylor, two different times from the city of Santa Maria acknowledging that this is the best natural healing place around after the hospitals. In fact, hospitals began to send their sick to the Healing Rooms.

After some months of living on the central coast of California and daily going into the Healing Rooms and daily being in the House of Prayer, I had never really asked for prayer for healing of my acid reflux condition. I just went to the Healing Rooms, and when I needed to I went and got a refill for Nexium. When it came time for my three-year endoscopy, this time the doctor came in and said, "You are fine. Go off all medicine." I actually thought to myself, "I must have been dreaming that."

I went to Dr. Hsia's office after all reports had come back. He looked at me again and said, "You are healed." He showed me his report, his pictures of everything working in my body. He said, "Your body is healing itself. You can now go off all medicine."

I left his office thinking, "Lord, somewhere between the Healing Rooms and the House of Prayer (which are all in the same building), You healed me. I didn't even think to ask You for healing, and You healed anyway." What an incredible testimony.

Therefore, I encourage you to always use the key—*cry out*. I might have gotten healed much sooner if I would have used this very key. *Cry out*. Just ask Him to heal.

This psalm has become a bookmark moment in my life for my healing. God gave me a creative miracle. I have been off all meds for acid reflux for four years with no signs of going backward, and I have much to praise the Lord about. He reached down and touched my body. He gave me a creative miracle. There was something missing in my body that I actually needed so that I could sing and praise and give thanks to Him. God reached His hands down and made something where nothing was. Therefore, I can pray and sing the words of David at the very end of Psalm 30. *I will give thanks to You forever*. Lord, You could never be praised enough. For all that You have done in my life, I could never praise You enough.

Here lies our final key for Psalm 30, and I am calling this, *thank You*. Take this key, *thank You*. Use this key every minute. Can we thank Him when we wake up in the morning? Can we thank Him all through the day? Can we thank Him for the little things and for the mighty things, for the creative miracles and the deliverances that He does in our life? Can we thank Him for the hope that He puts within us to call on His name and believe that God is who He says He is? He is our healing God.

The Wycliffe Bible Commentary writes, "No longer silent, the psalmist wants everyone to know of the change in his life—from mourning to dancing, from sackcloth to gladness, from silence to praise."[7]

I have found myself in the storyline of Psalm 30; you can too. I have been touched by the healer's hand, made whole through a creative miracle. Just retelling the story causes my faith to be stirred. The same will be true for you along with a newfound hope to believe that

He is *our* healing God. Can you pick up these keys? Keep them close and watch God work over and over in your life. He is our God of restoration, our God of deliverance, and our God who restores hope. We could thank Him multiple times a day, and just like David writes, "We could never praise You enough." Well, let's try.

DAILY PRAYER

Lord, I will exalt you and lift you high, for you have lifted me up on high! You made me to triumph. You make me to win. O Lord, my healing God, I cried out for a miracle and you healed me! You brought me back from the brink of death, from the depths below. You brought me back to life. And here I am, alive and well, fully restored. You are a miracle working God. You are a miracle healing God.

It looked like I was dying, falling into darkness, and You picked me up and You pulled me out. Every time I think about the Lord, every time I think about what He's done, I will give thanks? Oh Lord, thank You.

God, I've learned that Your anger lasts for a moment. I've learned that Your loving favor lasts for a lifetime. We may weep through the night, but at daybreak it will turn to shouts of joy.

So hear me now, oh Lord, and show me Your famous mercy. Oh God, be my Savior. You turn my mourning into dancing, removed my sackcloth, and clothed me with joy.

You crashed into my life when I was in the lowest place, You broke through. You transformed me, took my mourning. You said, "Here is joy. Take joy. Wear joy."

You pulled me out and set me on high, and I can never thank You enough.

Day 30: Write out Psalm 30

- This week, say this psalm out loud.
- Turn it into your prayer.
- Write this psalm down.
- Decree this psalm over your life.
- Be brave—sing it out loud.
- Can you remember the keys from this psalm?

Oh Lord, my healing God, I cried out for a miracle, and You healed me.

NOTES

1. David Guzik, "Psalm 30: Remembering the Greatness of God at a Great Event," The Enduring Word Bible Commentary, https://enduringword.com/bible-commentary/psalm-30.

2. Charles Spurgeon, *The Treasury of David*, "Psalm 30, verse 5," https://archive.spurgeon.org/treasury/treasury.php.

3. Julie Meyer, "I've Got The Joy," *Paint Your Picture*, https://www.juliemeyerministries.com/product/paint-your-picture.

4. Abraham Ibn Ezra, *Commentary on the First Book of Psalms* trans. H. Norman Strickman, (Brookline, MA: Academic Studies Press, 2009), 214.

5. Joseph Meyer, formerly a Doctoral Fellow in Classical Languages and Literature at UCSB.

6. Spurgeon, *The Treasury of David*, "Psalm 30, verse 2."

7. Pfeiffer and Harrison, *The Wycliffe Bible Commentary*, 506.

About Julie Meyer

JULIE MEYER is a popular worship leader and speaker, a Dove-nominated singer/songwriter, and an author. Julie is on staff at the Healing Rooms Apostolic Center in Santa Maria, California. She has an online community called Into The River that enjoys endless soaking worship, weekly Bible studies, and live interactive classes. Find out more at intotheriver.net